STO

9/25/01

ACPL ITEM

DISCARDED

3 1833 04058

S0-CHH-454

Five Stars for Managers

Five Stars for Managers
Strategy Concepts in Business

Herman S. Napier
Walter L. Kreeger

Purdue University Press
West Lafayette, Indiana

Copyright © 2001 by Purdue University. All Rights Reserved.

05   04   03   02   01   5   4   3   2   1

⊗ The paper used in this book meets the minimum requirements of American National Standard for Information Sciences—Permanence of Paper for Printed Library Materials, ANSI Z39.48–1992.

Printed in the United States of America

Library of Congress Cataloging-in-Publication Data

Napier, Herman S., 1922–
   Five stars for managers : strategy concepts in business / Herman S.
   Napier, Walter L. Kreeger.
      p.   cm.
   Includes bibliographical references.
   ISBN 1–55753–222–2 (alk. paper)
   1. Strategic planning.   2. Business planning.   I. Kreeger, Walter
L., 1944–.   II. Title.

HD30.28 .N368   2001
658.4′012—dc21

                                          2001019352

Contents

— 1 —

Sword Fighters and Pieces of Gold

A.D. 1600, Edo, Japan

The young Samurai looked at the coins on the merchant's table. He knew they were used for trade; their value was not his concern. He was not wise in the ways of money; he was schooled in the use of the sword—a long sword—and sworn to an oath of its unquestioned service—to death, if need be. He had little use for worldly possessions and, in his own way, felt a certain pride in not knowing the merchant's coins. The world of business and commerce was a strange and ugly land to him, full of greed and selfishness, unworthy of a warrior's regard.

By the time the Samurai and the merchant came into existence, the fighter and the craftsman-trader had already worked at their specialties for thousands and thousands of years. We must visit the Stone Age to see where it all began.

A Land of Sharpened Stones

Imagine we are in an airplane high above the mountains in eastern Europe. The glaciers are far to the north and the weather is cool but still fair. It is approaching 20,000 B.C. We expect soon to be near a primitive clan-village, and we hope that our guess of the location

1

is correct. With only two or three human beings per square mile, if we are very far off, we could spend most of our time looking for a village to visit. We assume that we will have to learn most of what we can by observation; there is little or no opportunity to study a native language.

For this project we have read any and all information available. Searching the landscape from the plane's window, we see smoke rising, reminding us that these natives are users of fire. Now we can see a group of shelters pitched on a rise in the valley floor near the base of the hills. We suspect that there are nearby overhangs or caves providing protection for the inhabitants. We also suspect that there might even be caverns for secret rituals.

We can see a flash of sunshine reflecting from the water of a narrow stream; the village is probably near a watering place well known to the clanspeople and to the animals inhabiting the area. In the distance, where the stream enters the lake, there appears a bog or a swampy area. The larger animals would have difficulty crossing this terrain, but others along with the clan might use it as a migration route.

Once on the ground, we shall have to appear friendly and unarmed. The spear-bearing males approaching our landing site seem to be driven by curiosity, just as we are. No doubt their descendants for generations will retell the story of a strange craft and its unusual people that visited their camp.

As near as we can tell, the social structure among clanspeople is well advanced and dominated by a male village chief or by a medicine man. Everyone knows his or her position, rules seem to be well established, common resources are shared, and certain visitors are welcomed by the clan.

The clan-village is actually more modern than we expected. Compared to ages in the past, the daily struggle for survival seems much easier now, and the pattern of everyday living is surprisingly complex. An animal that was once hunted solely for food is now used to meet other basic needs of existence. Tools and weapons necessary for day-to-day survival are placed in burial locations for use in the afterlife.

The clan depends on such tangible items as food, weapons, and tools; however, we can see evidence of another resource—the mind. For example, they have discovered the concept of the social unit that combines the various efforts of the individual clansmembers. In times past they had found that if a few clansmembers would pull on the end of a vine together in the same direction at the same time, they could compound their efforts so that a group whose effort was properly guided might pull more than another group twice its own size. From this phenomenon they also came to realize that an important key to group success is the exchange of information. Signals used might be signs, grunts, or half-formed yells, but these are critical factors aiding in cooperation. The clan has just invented the team.

Many years of practice and countless generations have given the hunter great skill and improved ability to forage, but he still travels miles through the countryside in his constant search for game. As we see him and his big-game team in action, it becomes apparent that there is a need for expertise in several fields of knowledge, such as behavior of the many different animals (including humans), a careful study of the weather, and appropriate use of the terrain. A good hunter blends easily into the available ground cover and appears or disappears as if by chance. It is quite clear that he knows the advantage of careful movement, the value of total surprise and, no doubt, the use of proper action and good timing in the final killing charge. At the same time it is also easy to understand that both hunter and hunted will try to gain every possible advantage over the other. For either one it is a deadly game of alertness and wits, and they both seem to understand that only one side can win.

The craftsman at work in the village does not concern himself with the issue of death on a daily basis as does the hunter. His main concern is with changing the form of inert raw materials into better products that will improve the life of the clan. There is always a need for good tools other than weapons; for instance, a fishhook can help the clan as much as a throwing stick can and a basket can help as much as an axe.

The clan-villagers' daily existence is obviously quite different from ours when it is judged from a very narrow perspective. When a broader view of the situation is accepted, the difference is less marked than we think. It is true that today we can throw our spears farther and kill more animals (and men); we can even build much bigger shelters and travel at much faster speeds. Yet, when given these advantages and much more, we still have not found the solutions to all of our human problems, especially those regarding group dynamics. Modern technology is awe-inspiring, but in the realm of people's social behavior, it is strangely far from complete. A few examples from life in the Stone Age show us how far we have come.

Management and Strategy for the Mammoth Hunters

In its day, the mammoth was the largest animal on land. It was many times stronger than humans and had senses more finely tuned and greater speed when needed. The mammoth hunter did have an advantage in the form of high technology: a stone-tipped spear that could be deadly, a flint knife that was very effective, and a very complex brain. If we were thrust into his situation today, our reaction might be to look in the Yellow Pages for a course in hunting big game. Certainly, at the very least, we would look for expert opinions on the basic concepts to master, starting with how to survive. If we could find a veteran from the Ice Age, it would not be hard to imagine what type of advice he might give:

1. Try to see every side of the situation. You must keep the big picture in mind and how all the pieces fit together—the last thing you want is a surprise. You should know the entire area in which you are hunting, paying particular attention to places that can cause problems so that you will know how to gain the advantage. You have to learn the nature of the beast you are hunting—know all of its capabilities. Study the climate and weather conditions and how they affect your actions in different kinds of terrain. Finally, you want the best weapons you can find and you want to be highly skilled in their use.

Once you know the general conditions and the obvious details, you can begin to search for those things not so easily seen. Experienced mammoth hunters know that the picture is never complete. Even with the best of efforts, a few things will be overlooked, and smart hunters know that you pay for what you don't see. But the hazard of missing important details is only one part of the problem. After thinking of all the different possibilities, you try to guess how each one of these will have an impact on something else. You can be sure that no single item by itself will account for the many things that are always waiting to happen.

Another key factor is learning to estimate instantly what the conditions might be, keeping in mind that all creatures engaged in this contest are always thinking and on the move. The best ones will try to anticipate the acts of the others.

2. Remember, you are a part of a team. A mature mammoth is much taller than a man, is many times as wide and long, and is protected by a thick hide covered with coarse hair. It has powerful weapons for attacking as well as for defending. With its trunk it can easily defeat the much-feared cave lion. Killing such a huge and powerful animal takes more than some accurate spear throws and strong arms; the good hunters will seek the advantage through teamwork. Even the biggest mammoth cannot be in two places at the same time, but a group of hunters divided into teams can attack from several sides to bring the behemoth down.

Aside from the team's ability to strike from different vantage points, the group has a much wider range of abilities than does an individual working alone. The group can see a problem from several different perspectives and search through a number of solutions. There are more hunters to watch for mistakes and to alert the team to new dangers. The knowledge of stalking and appropriate killing methods is very important for an individual working alone, but hunting the mammoth requires good teamwork.

The best team of mammoth hunters also realizes the need for good leadership. The chief hunter must display his commitment to both the team and the task. If he happens to be the most skilled hunter in the group, so much the better, but he must also understand the behavior of the mammoth and the behavior of his group. The best leaders are often the bravest people who set the highest standards for themselves and others. The same leadership required in mammoth hunting is also used in the village life of the clan.

3. Decide what you want to accomplish. Is the ultimate purpose of the hunt to kill the largest mammoth, or is it just to get food for the clan? There could be a good reason for either; you may not need to do both. The task of every mammoth hunt must first be understood in its broadest terms and then broken down into its basic components.

One approach to solving this problem is to think of the subtasks in the order they may appear. This can often be best accomplished by: a) describing the reason for the hunt, e.g., getting meat and raw materials; b) evaluating the means available, such as hunters and spears; c) deciding details of the actions, such as finding, killing, dismembering, and transporting. In effect, a good plan will include the objectives that are to be reached, the resources on hand to reach them, and the actions that will bring objectives and resources together.

In killing only one mammoth, the hunter team may plan to attack the beast at the place it is found, working on the assumption that the local conditions will be as good as they can be at the time. In a different situation, the team might wish to look for more information before a decision is made. There may be evidence that the animal has sensed the hunters' intentions and is watching or is even ready to charge. In still another situation it may be best to move the beast to a different location for a better plan of attack. Whatever the situation or the actions, there will always be ample hazards, and hence the operation needs careful planning.

In the actual killing phase, a team might choose to guide the beast to a cliff and then spook it into jumping. Another team might decide to force the animal into a section of wetland, where its movement would be greatly hampered and less likely to cause the team harm. A similar effect might be achieved with a very narrow canyon, a sinkhole, or a pit dug by the team. The emphasis is always on maximum gain for the hunters and minimum risk for the team.

4. Everyone must know the plan. Each team member should be able to answer the question, "What are we trying to do?" One group of hunters, for example, might set out to capture wild horses, intending to keep them for later, while another team may want the animals as an immediate food source. Either team could corral the horses, but their actions would not be the same. In other words—ensure that the group always knows just *what* it is trying to do (e.g., kill a mammoth), and also *how* it is to be done (e.g., driving it over the cliff). If the animals are to be moved to some other place for killing, the method of herding (e.g., distraction by waving fire torches, making strange sounds, etc.) must also be thoroughly discussed.

Clarity in explanation can eliminate misunderstandings later. Simple stick models, sand or cave drawings, and in some cases even more extensive visual aids may be used. It is possible that the use of such aids may account for drawings found deep in Ice Age caves, reminding us of "war rooms" for early planners.

Another important aspect of planning deals with priorities, such as the amount of attention given to the order of resource use and the sequence of actions. Prioritizing in such a manner is especially important when one considers limited means available, the different skills of team members, as well as the obvious items, such as the preferred weapons and tools. A common run of actions in a mammoth hunt could be a) finding a likely animal, b) killing it, c) cutting it into pieces, and d) protecting the booty and carrying it home. The assignment of priorities in such a case would seem rather simple. The most skilled hunters and the best weapons should be assigned to the killing phase, since, if the killing is not done in an efficient manner, the team may be subjected to additional effort and needless danger. Since finding the mammoth requires the skills of good scouts and not necessarily the best weapons or tools, a great number of men are usually not required to complete this initial phase. On the other hand, less attention to assignments is needed in the transportation phase—every member can carry some part of the load or help watch to protect the team.

5. Prepare for maximum effect. Halfway measures can be very hazardous, and it is often more desirable to overdo things the first

time than to risk failure of a project. There are times when re-hearsals are necessary to show that everyone is familiar with the key tasks and that weapons are in good condition. Be prepared to use every available resource, and make sure you can finish the job.

6. Learn all you can from mistakes—yours or anyone else's. Did the last hunting venture succeed? Did they bag an impressive trophy without losing any hunters? Spend some time thinking about how to improve the next hunt.

A very wise man—maybe an old mammoth hunter—once said that we don't learn much from the things we do right, we learn from the things we do wrong. Mistakes do carry their own form of punishment and are often etched quite vividly into our memories. The hardest lessons continue to teach us over the longest period of time.

We are still confronted with another problem: How do we really know when we have performed to the maximum? There are so many important factors involved that we always wonder whether we can actually measure success. It is probably a "gray-colored yes." The testing starts with the statement of purpose and looks at the means and the action, but the final outcome is always the gauge of a plan. For the mammoth hunter team, a good start (e.g., finding suitable game) is a commendable act; but a good finish (e.g., killing it and bringing it home) is the ultimate test.

A completely successful performance is seldom, if ever, achieved, because any group effort is complex and is never easy to judge. Heady applause might come quickly if a hunter team were to kill the much-feared cave lion; but if one man was killed in the process, it would certainly be far from their finest hour. The real concern is whether they come back with the prize at the lowest possible cost to the team and not with glowing reports of all the big ones they happened to see on the way.

7. Finally, the hunter must look ahead to see what could happen next, first in the immediate area, and then at greater distance. As a part of any planning, the unexpected must somehow be expected, and the team must be ready to implement the alternate plan. The best mammoth hunter must have a keen sense of his surroundings and adapt his actions where appropriate. He must be

aware of his opponent, a strong and unforgiving adversary, and any surprise may be disastrous.

The discussion has now turned full circle. Being aware of the entire situation allows the mammoth hunter to be ready for instant change. The hunter knows that a change starting in one area is indicative of changes in other areas. A small deviation from the initial plan may appear as a minor event, but viewed in the bigger context, we see that the entire situation has changed. The old hunters are still around because of their ability to meet impending threats. In the back of their minds was a little reminder that other predators are also out there, waiting and watching for game.

The Craftworker's Version

The village craftsman's work is judged on whether he makes a quality product, and not on how far he can throw it. The stone axe he makes is judged on whether it stands up to hard use, and a blanket of skins he makes is judged on whether it can keep out the cold.

If the toolmaker could add to what has already been said about the hunter, he probably would say the following:

1. The hunter's realm is the whole countryside, but the craftsman's attentions are mostly limited to what he finds on the ground. He may visit the same area as the hunter, but with a different focus; instead of looking for a moving animal, his targets could be rocks, bones (e.g., discarded set of antlers), or a particular kind of wood. An awareness of the whole area is always important to the craftsman, but detecting changes and movements may not be that critical. When he has found the raw material from a once-living creature, his own safety is not a major concern. All that remains now is for him to bring it home.

2. The concept of teamwork is critical for mammoth hunters for nearly every task on almost every outing; however, the craftsman's idea of a group effort is still a bit more abstract. Society and its many subgroups are important to him, but his role is more solitary. Later he will attract helpers and eventually apprentices and then will begin an exchange of ideas with other craftworkers.

3. Prior planning is always a good practice in either hunting or in crafting. The craftsman's task is to find the raw material, change its form, and adapt it. The hunter has a somewhat similar problem, but it is complicated by the object of his activities, the team of hunters themselves, and the dynamics of the hunt itself. Because the craftsman has more control and flexibility in how he conducts his work, his hazards are greatly reduced. If he decides one day not to look for new materials, he can work from his stockpile from previous outings. Most of the items he makes (e.g., an axe, a bowl, a medicine bag) do not have to be replenished on a regular basis, as do food and water. Therefore, if he already has a successfully designed product, such as a knife or a scraper, he can improve upon his technique. Because his products do not have to be replenished or redesigned on a daily basis, the work of many later artisans (e.g., musicians, composers, etc.) would not be given a high status in this society. Because the job is sedentary, the community expects a praiseworthy effort.

4. Ensuring that everyone understands how a particular task is performed is not that critical in craftwork except, of course, when the master accepts an apprentice. The effort is more one of showing an accepted method, and then giving the student some on-the-job training. A broken stone or a damaged bowl is not a wounded mammoth; the hazards are obviously not the same.

5. The serious craftsman is likely to encounter the principles of preparation and maximum effort in his own special way. Motivation is generated internally rather than externally, and the action both mental and physical. The craftsman's risks for life are not like those of the hunter, and as the various activities multiply with the passage of time, extra training is required, thus reducing risk for life or limb even further.

6. The advantages of learning from one's mistakes apply to everyone. As the centuries pass, new dimensions of the craftsman's work appear, as do the interests in barter and trade. As long as only a few products are exchanged, there are few trading problems; but with greater numbers and diversity in products, the complexity becomes more apparent.

3 1833 04058 7088

7. Looking into the future, we can imagine a time when conditions faced by the craftsman (as merchants or service providers) will become as complex as any of those of the hunter—both will have large teams in the field. Eventually, the craftsmen and hunters will face the same human problems: What does it take to understand our fellow workers, and how can the common goals be obtained?

Some Fighters Use Paper and Gold

Our mammoth hunter from the Stone Age was a highly skilled professional; he could meet and overcome any animal that roamed the earth. As early as 20,000 B.C., the concept of the killer team was already highly developed. Unfortunately, even then it was probably used to kill other men. The descendants of the old hunters had found that the experience gained in hunting could also be used to drive other groups from their lands or even enslave those who refused to leave. The old killer teams, first honored for their bravery and hunting abilities, now came to form their own nobility—a privileged warrior class. Such an aristocracy, based on violence and conquest, did bring a measure of order to life in the countryside, even though that order came in the cloak of warfare. In the process of building new fighting units, fiefdoms soon came to learn that fielding an army is costly, the land is stripped, and the common people must endure greater hardships.

The craftsman developed into a successful trader and factory manager, but he was still despised by the warrior nobility and ranked low on the social order. But time brought change with the creation of a barter system. This system was as critical for the craftsman as was the team concept for the hunter. But still another notion was to come, one that would not only simplify trade but would change its practice forever. It altered the details of trade from exchanging products for other products (e.g., one ox for twenty spearheads) to the trading of products for money. Shiploads of cattle or baskets of grain no longer had to be moved to the place of trade and only small items of equal value could be exchanged there instead. While land continued to be a major source of wealth and influence for the warriors, the merchant now had a method to develop his own kind of power. Under the new system he could arrange for quicker shipment and transfer of expensive goods, even the weapons and supplies for large numbers of soldiers. Now he also had a unique source for gaining wealth and power over people, even the warrior class. Differences in rank and influence between members of the warrior aristocracy and the rich traders were becoming less noticeable. Each one now had the weapons for social influence; their tools were, respectively, the warrior's sword and the merchant's coin.

More than a thousand generations have lived since the days of the clan-village hunter and craftsman. Now it has become more difficult to find a significant difference between leading soldiers and directing workers in crafts. The general management activities of their organizations can be described with different expressions, but the concepts that serve to guide them seem to be the same: define the mission and major objectives, assemble the various resources, and plan a series of actions. It may be fitting to examine the old management question: Are the concepts from long-ago hunters-turned-warriors of value in commerce today? Or, queried from the other side: Could the methods of modern merchants be useful in waging a war? Who is really the king of the mountain, or is either one destined to be? At least one part of the question can be answered. The mountain king will always be the one who gains the most from studying human organization, its theory and practical application, its structures, its possible strategies, and how a manager can succeed in facing a changing world.

Which One Is the Merchant's Child?

Over time, the skills of the hunter-turned-warrior and those of the craftsman-trader had been combined to make better weapons of metal, and even faster chariots that changed the shape of the world. In the Middle East, by 700 B.C., Assyria had developed a military and political organization to integrate the best work of its craftsmen into factories and the support of its traders to aid the nation at war. The governments of the Greeks and the Romans used every able-bodied citizen, whether craftsman, trader, or farmer, to serve in their military forces. A few, like the Roman Cincinnatus, in the fifth century B.C., would go from a warrior's role to that of a peaceful farmer, be called back to the role of dictator, and finally return to the plow.

As time moved on, it became more difficult to separate the war of business from the business of war. By the 1600s the English and Dutch East India trading companies were traveling the seas with soldiers hired to guard their shipping routes and to protect the sources of goods. Troops from the English company under the command of Robert Clive would eventually confront the French trading company and its allies at the Battle of Plassey (1757) and gain a victory in India that would set the stage for many years of dominance by the British Empire. In other areas there was also increasing evidence of business involvement in the efforts of war. In the late 1600s, for example, it was common for a European regimental commander to obtain a permanent commission to serve in his country's army, where he was provided revenue from the king for the number of men he recruited, along with extra payment for military equipment and supplies. By careful budgeting (e.g., hiring men for only one campaign at a time) he could assure himself of a steady income; and when he came to retirement age, he could sell his commission to another enterprising newcomer.

Other cases can be found that combine the concepts of business and warfare. During the Thirty Years' War, Albrecht von Wallenstein, a businessman, proposed that he be given a contract to recruit an army of 50,000 men that he would personally lead to defeat the Danish invaders and drive them from German soil. He would do this at no cost to the government—booty would be his pay and reward. The offer was accepted as stated, and Wallenstein did exactly what he said he would do.

Wallenstein and the business-like regimental commanders of Europe were not unique in combining the talents of commerce and the military. Numerous others have shown such abilities in the

United States. Before the Civil War began, Pierre G.T. Beauregard was an officer in the U.S. Army but was also a native of Louisiana and, like Robert E. Lee, chose to resign his commission to serve with the Southern cause. Beauregard commanded the troops who fired on Fort Sumter, the incident that started the war. He moved up rapidly in grade and, before the years of fighting were over, finished his military career as a general of highest rank. Unfortunately, after the war, such a title was a disadvantage. Former Confederate army officers were viewed as outcasts by the national government, and many had difficulties in making the postwar adjustment. By 1865, Beauregard, 47 years of age, had no income when he decided on a business career. As his first position he accepted the job of rebuilding the New Orleans, Jackson, and Mississippi Railroad. Most of the rolling stock and track system had been destroyed or badly damaged during the war years, but the former general's tireless efforts soon put the line back into operation. Trains were again running on a regular schedule, new revenue was being generated, and improvements were made in management. In April 1866, Beauregard was made president of the company, a position he held until 1870, when the system was acquired by another railroad. Through his efforts to rebuild the company, the former army general came to be a highly respected corporate manager, one of the top businessmen of his time.

Nathan Bedford Forrest was already a successful businessman in Tennessee when the Civil War broke out. Like Beauregard, he was looking for his own way to serve the Southern cause. Since he had no previous military experience, he decided to solve the problem in a typically direct fashion by joining the ranks as a private. The year was 1861, and he was already 40 years old. Fortunately for the Confederate army, his "private" status did not last for long. Forrest's potential was soon recognized, and he was persuaded to leave the ranks and form a regiment of his own. By the time the war was over, he was a lieutenant general and considered one of the most outstanding officers in the Confederacy. If a lack of prior military experience and ignorance of military history were major disadvantages, it did not show in his ability to frustrate Northern generals. General Sherman, who ranked second only to Ulysses S. Grant, called him "that devil Forrest." In a comment made after the war, Sherman declared the Tennesseean to be the most remarkable man to have served on either side.

By the end of World War I, Robert E. Wood had risen from the rank of lieutenant of cavalry to brigadier general and Acting Quartermaster General of the U.S. Army. He was about 40 years of age in 1919, when he decided to return to civilian life. He was soon hired as a senior executive in the firm of Montgomery Ward. While he had no business background to boast of, he did have some definite opinions on what corporate strategy should be. From his study of changes in the population, he was convinced that the greatest opportunity for Montgomery Ward lay in the retail stores. Unfortunately, his views did not coincide with those of the company's management and not many years passed before Wood resigned from his job. In 1924, Julius Rosenthal, the chief executive of Sears, Roebuck and Company, hired General Wood as a vice president. Four years later, Wood was president of the firm. During his term as president, and later as the chairman of the company's board, Robert Wood was usually given credit for making Sears, Roebuck and Company one of the largest retailers in the world.

General Wood was not the only senior officer in recent times to shift to a business career. A number of World War II generals later served in top management positions. One of the most outstanding of these was General Lucius D. Clay, whose last army assignment was as Military Governor of Germany. After his retirement in 1949, there were many suggestions that he run for political office, and he had offers of high executive rank in a number of corporations. Instead, he chose to accept a position with a small paper company in North Carolina. About two months later the company was purchased by a large defense contractor and, to avoid any conflict of interest, General Clay asked for release from his job. His real management opportunity came some time later, when he was approached by a member of the board of the Continental Can Corporation. The company chairman felt that the firm had become too centralized and was interested in the general's views on restructuring. In 1950, Lucius D. Clay, at the age of 53, became chairman of Continental Can's board of directors as well as its chief executive officer. At that time the company was second in size to the American Can Company by almost one-third. Six years later, under Clay's leadership, Continental Can passed American Can in profits, and by 1959 was the unquestioned leader in the packaging industry. It may well have seemed strange to its stockholders that the leading can company in the United States was led by a former military man with no civilian experience. In an interview, General Clay once said that he saw little difference between the army and business, except that "the test in business is more immediate. It's that little figure in the lower right corner that you have to watch." During his service at Continental Can, Clay was acknowledged to be one of the most outstanding business leaders in the United States.

The swordsman of old Japan is only a distant memory; the Wallensteins of Europe today seek only to drive their business competitors, not armies, back to the sea. It is easy to forget that those Stone Age hunters and many of those who followed them still cast their long shadows on the shifting scenes of the present and the broad expanse of ideas that tell what the future might be.

The insights of great chieftains of times past can still give inspiration to the businessperson of the present day, but he or she must be willing to study the old world as well as the new. The forward-looking executive, keeping the past in mind, is one who is ever alert to new opportunities, no matter where they may be. The executive must always start with the broadest possible outlook and remember that everyone who thinks like a general does not necessarily have to wear stars on a cap.

— 2 —

Look at the Big Picture First

Nobody wants to retreat, much less give the order to do so; however, on that one day there was no other choice. It was especially bad for Pickett's division—the general could see the dead and wounded around him—there were no more troops to call in. His men and the rest of the Army of Northern Virginia had paid a terrible price in losing the battle at Gettysburg—the cost was 20,000 men. It was a tactical reverse of the first order.

This loss was also a strategic setback. If General Lee and the Southern forces had been able to defeat the Union army in its own territory (less than 100 miles from Washington), he could have earned new respect for the Confederate efforts, inspired greater financial support from the Europeans, and, quite possibly, changed the outcome of the Civil War. The Battle of Gettysburg left its mark on the entire American population and its supporters. It also affected their views on the future of the South. In strategy, a commander must look beyond the battlefield and the destruction of troops and materials.

An Eagle Sees More Than a Fox

Ideally, one learns the key patterns of a puzzle and then fits the pieces together. This is seldom easy to do. A good field commander studying the terrain of the battlefield is constantly engaged in self-debate in an effort to solve the problems of combat. The commander looks far beyond the nearby wood lots and cattle fields, the hills, the wide valleys and streamlines that everyone else will see. A good business executive also does much the same; he or she is well aware of the local scene but looks beyond to more distant possibilities and how they will have an impact on future plans.

The army commander tries to examine as much of the battle area as possible, but should not fly so high or stray so far afield that he loses his contact with the fighting troops. The true strategist maintains an open mind for an array of possibilities. He cannot make plans without evaluating the threats and opportunities around him, and he cannot start an operation without knowing precisely where his units are and what they are able to do. He is constantly confronted with the problem of balancing gains and losses, knowing the battle's environment, and controlling the action at hand. His viewpoint is ever changing; first the broad scope, then near focus. Finally, he tunes the action to the situation at hand.

The ground commander first examines the weather, the terrain, and the intelligence on enemy strength and location. The weather can hamper observation and troop mobility, and the terrain becomes a three-dimensional gameboard with mountains, valleys, and roadways that can be natural approaches to objectives or become problems for unit movements. To see these from only one perspective is never enough; the advantages change with the view. It is easy to find the fields of a mountain or farmland or to mark the rivers and towns. Anyone can locate the cities and road nets, the airports, the factories and swamps. The strategist must know how these will aid or impede the movement of troops and how the use of available firepower will increase or lessen the impact of enemy actions. The analysis is never finished; it only starts over again.

The strategist cannot build his case from the details; he must start with the biggest picture. If he began with the smallest section, he would be like the groundhog attempting to describe a city—his viewpoint would be too restricted. The woodchuck really has a different problem; he is limited in cranial capacity and mobility. The human strategist has the mental advantage, but man and rodent still have the same amount of time when trying to collect information.

Although any strategist must first cast a wide look at the countryside, he is never excused from observing the details. The important thing in the process of looking at the countryside is the order in which it is done. It must start with the broadest possible view, because this puts the entire scene in perspective. It is a mental dialogue that starts with an examination of the situation from a wide scope to show the parts and to bring the relationships into focus. Then the details may be filled in. The view must once more take in the larger picture to see where the relationships may have changed. Starting this process with the details can shed light on the local conditions, but it does not reveal patterns of change. If your only view of combat is through a telescope, you may well forget to guard the back of your head.

A battlefield commander looks first at the general situation; he reviews his statement of mission, determines the objectives that must be reached, and examines the resources at hand for the task. He narrows down the problems and solutions in each area; then backs off and studies the impact of the mission on the task at hand. U.S. generals are not unique in this. Some generals from North Vietnam gave us an example during the late 1960s of how the process (wide scan, detail, then re-scan) might have been used as part of their strategy in the south. Looking at the broad picture of the war, they apparently questioned whether their troop strength was enough to defeat the enemy ground troops and, at the same time, neutralize the air force bases. If the Viet Cong as small units were able to destroy the airfields, the scattered units of ground troops could come together again and continue the war on the ground. On the other hand, if the American and South Vietnamese ground troops were defeated first, the airfields, now alone, would soon become untenable and probably fall by themselves. The North Vietnamese generals chose to concentrate their efforts on fighting the troops on the ground.

Business writers often give the same advice as does the military—only in different words. They advise us to look at our company from the viewpoint of serving its major contributors: the customers, the workers, and the investors. They then advise us to compare these activities to those pursued by competitors. As always, such things may seem easy enough when articulated in text, but they are not quite as easy to implement. One energy-oriented company in the United States apparently felt it was competent enough to handle management problems in a different field of endeavor and hence acquired a large retail chain. Most of the target company's managers were kept in place, but strategy for the new conglomerate was set by the energy masters. Unfortunately, these executives had little retail experience, and the merger did not succeed. After only a few years, the badly battered retailer was back on the auction block.

Information Is the Fuel for a Plan

The top manager of a company may have a good grasp of the situation. He may even know the key areas he must study and be quite certain of the sort of information he will need. Finding that information, however, can still be a problem. Karl von Clausewitz, in the 1820s, wrote of the "fog of war"—the uncertainty that always exists—that "circumstances press for immediate decision and allow no time for a fresh look around, often not even enough for careful consideration." A leader of the smallest combat patrol may show a high state of alertness and yet make the poorest guess at the strength of an enemy force. Even a corps commander could be at a similar disadvantage as he tries to explain the slow movement forward of his widely scattered divisions. Clausewitz finally came to conclude that when one is exposed to battle conditions, impressions from the senses may be much more powerful than any force of ideas that results from careful thinking. It is easy to be misled, and it is more pleasant to hope than to think. He also came to believe that the reliance on one's own convictions and the laws of probability are the best guides for thought and action. Napoleon once remarked that a general never knows anything with certainty—it is with the "eyes of the mind" that he sees, knows, and judges the situation.

Even when the information appears to be adequate, some critical facts may be missing or not available. Information that was obtained at an earlier time may be invalid at the time of the briefing or even unsuited for the action plan. Simplified assertions have greater appeal than a complex statement of truth; vivid impressions become more convincing than facts. Military writers may stress certain important factors, such as key features in the terrain or dispositions of enemy troops, but a hundred genies still work to confound the issue. Aside from all this, a single report on the progress being made may give encouragement, while two additional reports may well raise greater uncertainty. Even with the most serious efforts, the memory of a few past errors can certainly put doubt in our heads. Wrong or incomplete information has forced many attacks to start at inappropriate times or places. The lack of good information has, time and again, resulted in a failure by commanders to perceive enemy blocking positions, danger areas, and enemy actions. In business, misjudgment of a market's potential can be caused by poor reporting; mistakes in sales forecasting are common when improper data are employed. Such errors have resulted in products being manufactured but not sold or that have to be sold at a loss. Greater costs probably result from a lack or misuse of information than from all other causes combined.

Often the best skill for the strategist is a good imagination combined with some guesswork. Time and space are so vague that they can never be observed directly, and so, perception becomes one's reality. The formulation for any strategy means sketching a composite picture from a mixture of many impressions. Even with these difficulties, a prudent manager tries to ensure that key factors are analyzed and cross-analyzed so that nothing is overlooked. Nearly 2,500 years ago, Sun Tzu summarized the problem when he said, "Now the general who wins a battle makes many calculations in his temple ere the battle is fought. The general who loses a battle makes but few calculations beforehand. Thus do many calculations lead to victory, and few calculations to defeat; how much more no calculations at all!"

The corporate chief executive officer does not have the task of looking for fighting units that hide in the woods, but his or her problems are just as taxing. With experience it may become easier to tell whether the important facts are being considered, but there will always be an element of uncertainty. Still, one's judgment can be improved with good thinking habits and practice whether one is in a battle or in the marketplace.

Habits can give an advantage, or they can lead to despair. They can guide us, cause us to assign an improper value to something important; or they can cause us to overlook other values. Habits can also lead to overconfidence, something that is shared by all of us. Even the world-renowned grand planners have shown their own feet of clay. Napoleon Bonaparte and Adolf Hitler, separated in their ambitious projects by over a hundred years, each appeared quite certain he could capture Moscow and bring Russia to its knees. They found this easier to say than to do. Napoleon took a few months to learn the lesson; Hitler needed two years.

Errors in judgment cost dearly—not only in military operations. The W.T. Grant company in the early 1970s made a series of debatable choices in their general management methods: new pricing and credit policies, the types of products to sell, and a number of other decisions. With more time for a careful review, they might have been able to recover from some mistakes, but conditions were not in their favor. The company had previously been one of the largest retailers in the United States. Five years later it was bankrupt, and today the firm no longer exists.

The manager of another U.S. company appeared to believe that it could make a quick profit by out-maneuvering the other suppliers of raw uranium materials. When costs turned out to be higher than expected, they attempted to back out, but it was too late. The resultant flurry of lawsuits sought nearly $2 billion, most of the assets of the firm. The great executives of Sun Tzu's time would have studied such examples with great care. No doubt they would have been quick to applaud overconfidence in the ranks of an enemy.

Deciding what is important in a complex situation is always difficult, but there are a few conceptions that need to be high on the list. For example, it seems almost axiomatic that, before anything else, the organization must survive as a unit; hence items affecting this condition must be given priority. If a defending unit has been surprised and is unable to move its reserves, success is suddenly moot: if cash is not ready to meet the payroll, a business will grind to a halt. Sun Tzu chose to put it another way when he wrote, "The good fighters of old first put themselves beyond the possibility of defeat." Napoleon remarked that the general, before looking at anything else, should make certain that his army is "vulnerable at no point." Their advice to a business executive would probably be much the same: Make ready for any adversity before you enter the contest. Ability to stay the course must be the first thing to check.

We can usually find a few other things to check. Chester I. Barnard, in his book *The Functions of the Executive,* aired the notion of a "limiting factor," one that is essential to a project's success. He explained that it may be as simple as a single bolt or a screw without which a piece of machinery would not run—or as complex as a body of technical know-how required for a specialized job. Any good decision maker puts forth a special effort to identify these factors, then he reviews the status of the system, time and again, to ensure that they are in place.

Once convinced that he has ample resources for the operation, including the latest information, a strategist would appear to have an advantage. Usually, it is not as great as he thinks. Time has a way of changing things; the future not only comes very quickly, it enters through many doors. We cannot assume that the capabilities of an army or business enterprise will always stay as they are. Even the old opponents and their habits may change. The best protection from the hazards of the unexpected is to anticipate what the future might be. The greater the number of possibilities considered, the less the chance of a surprise. While the outcomes may not match an expectation, the greatest error that can be made is never even to guess.

Fortunately, there are some good rules that help one to anticipate the future. In combat, one of the best policies is to deal in capabilities. Whatever the enemy *can* do we must assume he *will* try to do (do not try to guess his intentions—he can easily change his mind). No likelihood should be overlooked, not any action or place. At least one English king about 200 years ago might have chosen a different plan if he had considered the possibility that British regulars would not outlast the untrained farmers in the far-off American colonies.

Half-thinking Becomes Half-acting

Most of us learned a long time ago that when two things are viewed together, they are not the same as the items apart. Two gases (e.g., hydrogen and oxygen) can combine to form a liquid, and two liquids can turn into a solid. By the same token, knowing about black or white does not mean that you understand gray. A famous astronomer once remarked that when we are aware of two different concepts, we risk seeing one or the other, forgetting the "and" in between. It is not enough to know that fact A is affected by fact B, and B influenced by A; they are both altered just by the presence of other influences. The relationship is seldom confined to A and B influences—but also often includes C and D and even factors up to Z and beyond. In 1812, the French army finally did occupy Moscow, the capital and political symbol of Russia at that time, but the important supplies and equipment had been removed by the Russian army as it withdrew to the east. Napoleon had gained a significant objective but was left with a city in flames. Even worse, his army was not prepared to survive the Russian winter. Bonaparte's two greatest problems were 1) to endure the extremely cold weather, and 2) to defeat the Russian army. When he could not solve these two problems together, his only option was to retreat.

The North Vietnamese generals were also careful to mix the relevant concepts beforehand. They knew that if the U.S. forces could keep their units together, the ground troops would protect the air bases, and the air force could aid troops on the ground. The end result, by arithmetic, would be a $1(A) + 1(B) = 2$ situation and remain as it had been before. On the other hand, if the ground troops could be made ineffective, the mathematics could change. Then the *effects* of A could simply multiply with B and the formula give $0(A) \times 1(B) = 0$. The ground troops could probably survive without a major air force, but the reverse would seldom be true. In a business situation, money and manpower are A and B; when either of these is absent, the answer is also zero.

Napoleon is not the only decision-maker who has ever misjudged critical items and how they fit into a system. The managers of a large paint and wall-covering firm in the United States decided they could increase the company's profits with a major effort in sales. By raising the advertising budget and lowering the selling price they were able to attract more customers. Revenues increased, as expected, but other things did not come out as they should have. Sales went up more slowly than costs, and income went down. Instead of producing the expected additional profits, the A's and B's of the operation seemed to be acting in conflict, and the hopes of success were demolished.

Such examples are not mentioned to argue that the problems stated are simple, or that decisions are easy to make. Even when the critical factors are few, interactions are hard to control. Sun Tzu once observed that the art of war is governed by only five constant factors, and that all the different conditions come about due to these factors (the moral law, heaven, earth, the commander, and the method of discipline). He did not go on to discuss in detail how soon the situation becomes complicated. Basically, there seems to be no option but to study every part of the situation then to try to guess about the whole.

Theory as a Map in the Head

The strategic manager is, by definition, the original owner of the old sign, "The buck stops here." He is responsible for everything the organization does and whatever it fails to do. This also includes, of course, what might come in the future. He must try, without ceasing, to anticipate everything and to find the appropriate solutions. Fortunately, this is not always as difficult as it might often appear. A man who lives by the ocean's shore cannot alter the approaching hurricane, but he can do something beforehand to minimize the damage expected. At worst, people can leave the area and wait until the storm has passed. A chief executive can also look at the possibilities and study their probable impacts and then plan for the different conditions. Any business manager can choose a particular market segment and study its many aspects.

Study alone will not be enough, however. No matter how good his forecasting might be, the forecaster still must consider the action. This fact entails some new possibilities, which include setting objectives and standards, feedback of information, types of corrective actions, and gauging the final outcome.

Formulating and implementing an organization's strategy is always a difficult process, but it has already been done many times, and there are a number of guidelines for anyone willing to learn. As strange as it may seem, one of the best tools for such practice is good theory. The typical chief executive is not likely to think of himself as a theoretician, but this is how his actions can often be explained. Any time he brings a number of ideas together in an examination of what the company does or how it might generally function, he borrows a common implement long used by thousands of scientists. In a process that differs little from what the businessperson does, theoreticians try to use work from the field and laboratory to fit the pieces of their research into a usable plan. If their concept (theory) is well constructed, it amounts to a list of shrewd guesses (hypotheses) or a checklist of critical factors. A big advantage of this technique is that as it patterns ideas together, it can reveal logical errors in the theory that has been constructed.

For example, an examination of many military and business situations can lead to the conclusion that an interacting environment (E) sets typical conditions in which an organization (O) and its strategy (S) will succeed or fail in results (R). The basic conception can be stated in quite simple terms:

$$E \rightarrow O/S \rightarrow R$$

This theory/model is the key idea that must guide executive action. It can act as a military or business checklist in a wide range of hard (work) situations.

A better understanding of relationships may be gained with a somewhat different statement of the model:

$$\text{Environment} \rightarrow \text{Organization/Strategy} \rightarrow \text{Results}$$

Resources   Actions   Objectives

This format amounts to a simplified mental reminder for the decision maker to look at the external environment (physical conditions, competition, etc.), then at the organization and its strategy—from a viewpoint of resources available (personnel, finances, etc.), actions possible (attack, expand, etc.), and key objectives (take Hill 101, increase sales 20 percent, etc.). Finally one considers some different results (distance moved, assets gained, etc.) for progress evaluation.

In the U.S. Army, field manuals for staff and commanders give many instances of this type of theorizing. The manuals are commonly described as action guides or checklists. One well-known example is the commander's "Concept of Operation," typically presented in a planning meeting as a guide for the staff and commanders. Beginning with a general concept of the situation, the senior commander or manager can organize his thoughts on the major factors involved, on the sequence of activities, and on how one might best proceed.

An expanded version of the model just presented would consider a range of critical factors as explained in the chapters that follow. These include the elements of environment, organization, strategy, communications, actions, and results. The following discussion offers a brief introduction to each.

Environment.   There is a host of different impacts on any organization from the outside environment. Oversimplified, these comprise a range of threats and opportunities that the strategist will have to consider. These impacts include a number of physical, social, political, economic, and technological inputs that will be dealt with later in greater detail. At present we need to add one unique external factor that is too often taken for granted: that is the factor of time—one of the critical resources considered by any strategist. Even a project with an unlimited budget and staff is doomed if enough time is not available. In a military operation, if time is not available for a personal reconnaissance or some other study of terrain, the planning will be inadequate and the hazards and costs will be high. In business, if a lack of time prevents the analysis of market conditions or the training of key personnel, the resulting disadvantage will only bring good fortune to better-prepared competitors.

Once a strategy has been formulated, time must then be allowed for subordinate commanders or managers to receive and interpret the plan. One of the first questions any chief must consider is: How long do the lower units need to study the situation and make their own preparations? As larger units are considered, more factors and events intervene, and more time is also required. A business, compared to a military unit, may seem to operate in a much more placid environment, but there are still as many problems in that environment. For example, everyone must look to the basic question: How much time will be necessary for executing the strategic plan? Will one year be long enough? Two? Maybe it should be ten. An error in estimating how long it will take to develop and introduce a new product or in preparing an army to fight can turn out to be quite expensive. In business, the major cost is in dollars; in wartime, sadly, cost is in lives.

There is a long-standing argument among military historians that the slow movements of Count Grouchy at Waterloo may have cost Napoleon his crown. There are also business observers who claim that it took U.S. manufacturers too long—by ten years—to decide that the Japanese could be serious auto competitors. When General Motors and others decided to act, a big part of their market was gone. Time must be a major element in any strategy.

Organization.   The organization's strengths and weaknesses are a primary consideration in planning any strategy. We study the tangible assets of businesses or the arms and equipment of the military, along with the ages and backgrounds of the leaders, the morale and training of personnel, and numerous other items. Not to be overlooked here are the effects of the interactions that occur in the social environment where the working or fighting is done. An organizational "climate" soon develops for each worker. Each person's personality and leadership style contributes to the climate. Frederick the Great of Prussia was not only speaking to his generals when he told of the vivid impressions conveyed by a chief executive: "We all sense the captain's attitude and how he feels toward his men." The smartest of managers soon learn that it is very difficult to "fool the troops," either on the battlefield or on the factory floor.

Strategy.   If the organization's structure is a snapshot of jobs and their relationships, its strategy is its moving picture. This is a complex and dynamic pattern—an interaction of resources, actions, and objectives, all stressing a common goal. In a military situation, the strategy is summarized in the commander's concept, and used by the lower level commanders as a framework for their planning and actions.

The strategist, by evaluating the environment's impact and the organization's capabilities, attempts to gain the greatest advantage before the action begins. The intention is the same in all cases: focus the maximum strength against the opponent's weakness in order to dominate a part of the market, or a place in the combat zone.

The three elements already mentioned (Environment, Organization, and Strategy) are basic to planning a strategy. The next three (Communication, Action, and Results) change the focus to execution.

Communication.   The proper execution of a strategy first depends on the manager's ability to convey his or her thinking to others. Anyone can devise a master plan; we all build castles in the clouds. What no single person can do is be in every place at one time. Yet the purpose of the organization is to combine the efforts of many different individuals and groups and to coordinate their many actions in reaching a common goal. To accomplish this, the communications network stands out as a critical factor. It is designed to inform all those in the chain of command and to facilitate the exchange of information from inside and outside the firm.

Action.   In implementing a strategy, two principal actions of a chief executive are: a) to show personal interest in the operation and b) to encourage those executing the plan. While this may be stated simply enough, the hazards are many. A thousand activities have to be monitored and multiple actions supported. At the same time this is being accomplished, some of the vital information may be grossly misinterpreted, overlooked, not accepted, or even not believed. At other times that information may also be ignored by those who could gain the most from its use. Reducing such possibilities can lead to the use of letters and mail service, liaison officers or aides and multiple messengers, and a dozen other expedients. In spite of all such efforts, the most we can usually expect is a reduction of the errors we make.

Upon receipt of instructions from the ranking commander or manager, the local executives prepare their own plans of action. Though the general scene of activity may seem to have changed, the work of the senior managers, in many respects, may have just begun. They must now attempt to keep informed of local progress and review the many plans, which must then stay matched to their own. This monitoring of ongoing planning and operations is one of the most important activities undertaken by any executive. If the workers or troops do not know how to do the job or do not understand why it is to be done, then it can be stated with near certainty that the results will not be up to the mark. The only way the chief can be sure is to go and see firsthand.

Results.   As the execution of a strategy proceeds, the chief executive must continue to make early judgments about what the outcomes might be at any given time. Aside from what can be seen by personal visits to units, the manager is forced to anticipate what happens elsewhere from reports that describe past events. Time does not allow for the instant compilation of information on what happened a minute before; the details do not come back until later. The effect of all this is that judgments are constantly being made; the manager must somehow fill the gap between what was projected in the plan (e.g., occupy the objective) and what has already happened (i.e., the actual situation). The details of most events are not clearly known when considered by the chief executive. It is thus from experience or guesswork that he or she must decide what progress is being made and what further actions are needed. After these fine mental acrobatics have been performed, the executive must reexamine the whole situation for a new range of threats and opportunities. In the end, a judgment must be made as to whether the old strategy is still the best or if a change should be made.

For General Lee in northern Virginia the "broad scan, the close look, the long view, and review" habit of studying situations served him well many times on the battlefield. More than 100 years later, it probably helped another strategist to develop a winning concept for business. From a modest starting point in Arkansas, Sam Walton studied the retailing problem in the plains of middle America. By considering the location pattern of smaller towns, the action of major competitors, and the general lay of the countryside, he developed an approach to retailing that enabled him to be stronger at places being overlooked by most of the retail giants. When his strategy was put into action, Wal-Mart became the largest retailer in the United States and made its strategist and his fellow managers richer than many ever dreamed.

— 3 —

Don't Leave Anything Out

It is the year 1288 B.C. Recently, a sizeable army has been reported massing north of Damascus. The general in charge of the advance has already moved to establish a base near Beirut. He then continued to the north, stopping only briefly at Kamu.

The general has arrived at his present location after thirty days and a remarkable march of 400 miles from the southwest. His encampment is only a few miles south of Kadesh, on the Orontes River. Most of the area is under the control of Egypt, whose king and army commander on the scene is the mighty pharaoh, Ramses II. The king will shortly become engaged in the first battle recorded in any detail in known history.

Unfortunately, the Egyptian king is in unfamiliar surroundings and not ready for a major engagement. The battle will provide an excellent demonstration that the principles of war are well founded. The Hittite king, in opposition to Ramses, will make good use of the principle of security as well as the element of surprise as he leads the Egyptian into an ambush. It is here Ramses becomes vulnerable to the Hittite's application of the principle of concentration of effort. The importance of this principle will become more evident as Ramses moves forward with obvious disregard for security. His army will be spread thinly over a wide area, hence it will be difficult to coordinate and control. The Egyptians are fortunate that their king, an experienced fighter, has a competent chief of staff. In spite of his self-imposed disadvantage through lack of proper intelligence, Ramses will be able to recover from his errors and organize an effective counterattack. He will defeat a sizeable portion of the opposing army before the day's end. The next morning, the Hittite king will propose a truce, and a peace treaty will be accepted and signed before Ramses returns to Egypt. Ramses will become famous for building great temples and huge statues of himself, recording in stone an account of his bravery and exemplary conduct in battle.

A Closer Look at the Territory

An untrained observer, looking at the surroundings in which a military or business operation is conducted, may see little more than a mixture of landscape, people, and random activity. A perceptive commander or chief executive has an entirely different view. He or she automatically thinks of a series of mental screens and sorts through the babel of sights and sounds to find the information needed for making important decisions. This broad-based thinker begins with the critical factors. In military practice, the term used to describe this list is the *essential elements of information,* or EEI. Under most battlefield conditions, the EEI comprises information on the weather, the terrain, and an estimate of the enemy's capabilities to impede the mission's accomplishment.

Most of the items can be stated in either military (e.g., enemy) or business (e.g., competitor) terms with little or no loss of meaning. Some of the key elements of information are:

1. Area of operation (e.g., major avenues of approach in an attack, the civilian transportation networks or distribution systems)
2. Population and social factors (e.g., urban and rural inhabitants as sources of friendly agents, markets for the company's products)

3. Government agencies (e.g., major supporting bases, regulators of trade)
4. Economics (e.g., critical materials for military strategy, labor and capital for commerce)
5. Technology (e.g., a breakthrough in weapons development, advantage in product research)
6. Competition (e.g., from a variety of enemy forces, from other business practitioners)
7. The future, involving any or all of the above. Simplified, there must be an evaluation of anything that could have a significant impact on the strategy being considered.

Area of operation (physical environment).   Although it is possible (and probably more nearly correct) to view this as including the limitless sky above, earth below, and the air and water between, we choose to concentrate on a more limited view of the land in the area of operation. In a military situation, the most critical element (aside from the enemy army) is the terrain upon which the fighting takes place. Sun Tzu (ca. 500 B.C.) mentioned six different kinds of terrain (accessible ground, narrow passages, precipitous heights, etc.), and other writers have discussed the types of warfare appropriate for a variety of terrain conditions (e.g., desert, mountains, river crossings). Napoleon placed great emphasis on an analysis of the theater of operations. Frederick the Great spent considerable time in discussions on the military advantages and disadvantages of particular regions of a country. In his writings and instructions, he discussed the evaluation of avenues of approach into an enemy country, the proper location of supply points, defensive positions, and methods of reducing hazards or improving the means of security. He also elaborated on the advantages and disadvantages of operations in mountains, at rivers, and in defiles. He felt that the first action a commander in any campaign should take should be to obtain the best maps available. That commander should then study them over and over again. Both Frederick the Great and Napoleon made much of the *coup d'oeil*, or the ability to see "at a glance" the best military use of the terrain, and considered this to be a talent of outstanding general officers. A good military strategist or tactician soon develops a habit of thinking in terms of the terrain advantages and disadvantages of every region

It has been argued in recent years that American officers think too much in terms of the type of terrain that exists in northern Europe, where many important battles of World War II took place. The ground is generally open and rolling and lends itself to rapid movement by tank-infantry and artillery teams. By way of contrast, Korea has more mountains, and Vietnam more jungles and swamp land. Under these conditions, vehicular-mounted soldiers find it much more difficult to maneuver.

The actions necessary to control a section of landscape may not be first on the list of problems for a businessperson. The rise in many types of land, water, and air pollution problems, coupled with increasing world trade and awareness of geography, requires the businessperson to employ prudent use of space, time, and travel. A better knowledge of the terrain and weather conditions as they influence the movement of personnel and supplies is of prime importance to a good strategist—military or civilian. The fact that another firm is being subjected to the same conditions does not mean that there are no opportunities.

Historically, the military commander tries to control the higher elevations. Better protection, improved observation, and more information are the primary advantages that accrue from such control. The business manager's equivalent of high ground is more likely to be of a mental nature and is reflected in such activities as superior research and training of personnel. In combat, the best ground approach to an objective can help to conceal forward movement and lead to the weakest enemy positions. In commerce, the best entry into a market allows for research and effective sales activity before potential competitors can make plans to respond. The study of high ground (e.g., hills and mountain regions) in a business situation may not always lead to more sales, but the choice of a poor location (e.g., inadequate road nets, limited water resources, etc.) can make for a clear disadvantage. The manager of one steel plant on the Mississippi River, in discussing the high cost of transferring large amounts of materials, questioned whether his company would ever again build a plant that was not near water transportation. He had come to realize that his company could water-ship finished steel from his Arkansas plant to Pittsburgh cheaper than steel mills in Pennsylvania could deliver it within their own state by truck.

A common, often cited mantra for realtors and retailers is "location, location, location." For the chief executive, a better catch phrase would probably be "integrate, integrate, integrate." There seems always to be a problem in coordinating activities, and difficulties are often unnoticed until it is already too late. Once, a large food company with interests in Central America established a farming operation on a river bank upstream from a canning plant being built on the coast. The idea was that the farm would have the advantage of downstream water transportation, producing a considerable saving in costs. Both the farm and plant operations were supervised by experienced managers, so we may assume that the project was carefully studied beforehand. The day finally came when the two facilities were completed. As the harvest began, boats were loaded at the farm and moved easily downstream to the plant. However, as the shipping operation continued, the realization came that seasonal rains much further upstream were causing the river to rise in its banks. As the current grew stronger, the boats had difficulty returning to pick up the next load at the upstream end. This problem had not been foreseen. In review, it became apparent that the different elements (i.e., farm, downstream plant, the weather, and the river between) had all been examined individually, but the complex of elements had not been analyzed together; interacting, they came to foil an otherwise logical plan. For careful, thinking strategists, the lesson is quite clear: the planning of two or three separate operations is not the same as planning them all together. As John Muir and other environmentalists have said: Everything is connected to everything else.

Population and social factors. Good commanders and chief executives are aware of a long list of demographic and social characteristics of people that can have an impact on any management action. Most do not go to the extremes of Alexander of Macedon, who had his officers marry women from occupied countries, but we usually make some effort, especially in the United States, to recognize cultural traditions. Army intelligence officers and marketeers both study the patterns of regional customs, religion, education levels, and income, as well as the ongoing changes in lifestyles and varieties of leisure activities. Still, with the best of efforts, it is easy to overlook or misinterpret some important parts of the picture. In the Korean War of the 1950s, Chinese POW camp commanders were convinced that, because of civil rights violations in the U.S., African American soldiers would be easy to brainwash and convert to the communist side. It did not work out quite that way, of course. What the Chinese cultural experts did not seem to understand was that the Black soldiers, in spite of any wrongs they may have suffered at home, first thought of themselves as Americans. The error in judgment is not new—it is always very difficult to understand human nature. Henry Ford, in the 1920s, assumed that a one-model, one-color vehicle would be cheaper to build and cheaper to purchase, and therefore would be a more popular automobile. It didn't work. What he actually did was give the managers at General Motors, with their multiple styles of cars, an advantage. Ford never regained its leading position.

The chief executive who studies the characteristics of the customers has a big advantage, especially in gauging the mind of a group. If one knows the dominant nationality (e.g., Irish, German), the majority religion (e.g., Catholicism, Islam), and the region or general section of the country (e.g., South, Midwest), he already has a good start in estimating the population's attitude on society's common issues (e.g., work, family). Population factors such as these are grist for the mill of the marketeer and those who hire workers for plants, for bankers, and for investment analysts. They are good even for judging morale. Multiple factors are included in the cluster patterns that describe a particular social grouping. One highly publicized cluster of attitudes is that of the "middle class," often summarized in the Midwest as White Anglo-Saxon Protestant, or "WASP."

The basic functions in business (e.g., production, marketing, etc.), are very much the same in any part of the world, but the way things are done can vary widely from country to country as well as from region to region or even from state to state. While most such operations appear to be similar, the attitudes of the people are not. Americans, for example, tend to emphasize the rights of individuals; Japanese give more stress to the team. An American may be a local hero for protesting against the "establishment," but the Japanese worker would appear to be more comfortable when following company rules. During World War II, U.S. military commanders in the Pacific knew they would have difficulty taking Japanese prisoners if any member of a unit survived. In more recent times, American managers of firms in the Middle East have become more aware of the critical role played by religion in the way that business is done. In many parts of the world, there is no "middle class" in the usual sense that we use the term—there are only rich landowners, poor tenants, and very few people between. In such regions, there may be a surplus of workers for hire, but few are trained as managers. Plans for operations in these countries must include consideration of what the impact might be. Expenditures anticipating these problems before they occur is always money well spent.

Government agencies (e.g., major supporting bases, regulators of trade). Military commanders are likely to see the government as their basic supporter and guide. They would logically look on their own role as an instrument of the duly elected officials, though the government may have been, in many cases, established through violence and arms. The history can be quite confusing. In the 1600s, the English East India Company was a commercial venture, but it was often supported by military troops (e.g., for security of trade routes). But as competition grew and the company expanded its presence, it actually served as the government, and later as the government's agent. All this came about when the French East India Company was the economic competition. In 1757, their differences resulted in bloodshed at the Battle of Plassey. Here, forces of the English company, led by Robert Clive, defeated soldiers from the French company and their group of Indian allies. This victory gave the English company control of India, which they held until 1858, when the British government officially took control.

The typical American business executive probably sees the large number of government rules and regulations as burdensome and often an unwise restraint. He must see that his company complies with countless laws that have an impact on every sector of business. A short list of areas where such rules apply would include marketing (such as advertising practices), production or factory conditions (e.g., occupational safety and health), personnel (for example, equal employment opportunities), finance (e.g., disclosure rules). A longer list could add others (such as environmental protection, restraint of trade, etc.). Different interest groups seem able to exert pressure on the lawmakers, who then find it necessary to establish an almost endless number of regulations. Once a particular law is established, interpretations can multiply the different actions deemed necessary, which results in many conflicting sets of rules (e.g., those that are set by the government and those that hold in the market). The problem is further aggravated when a company is operating in different states or countries, where laws are seldom the same.

Adding to these difficulties are regulations specifically designed for the chief executive. Some time ago, military managers accepted that a commander is responsible for everything that takes place in the area of his job assignment, whether he sees what takes place or not. In business, the areas of management activity are not so clearly defined. A corporate chief executive is presumed to have responsibility first to the owners of the firm, and here the job is quite clear: the manager is paid to make a profit. However, in more recent times, some different views have emerged. Other contributors to the organization (e.g., customers, workers, citizens of the community, etc.) have found their own special advocates to high-light and argue their respective cases. The result is that the chief executive has a problem in deciding which group is to be given priority, the benefits they will receive, and how this will all be accomplished. The company board of directors may come to see these questions argued in the media or in courts of law.

Most chief executives try to work with interest groups outside the firm while simultaneously feeling pressure to produce more income for the investors and higher wages for the workers. A decision on the location of a new plant can be influenced by the effort of local government and its citizens to attract more business, the distance from the labor pool, and the markets the plant management is planning to serve. The chances of success are enhanced, for both the town and the firm, when the local school board makes an effort to accommodate new people, bankers work overtime to expedite loans, and politicians give tax advantages.

Economics (e.g., critical materials for military strategy, labor, and capital for commerce).   When Clausewitz wrote that war is an extension of national policy, he could have added that economics, as well as politics, influences an extension of war. Large amounts of human and material resources are mobilized during national emergencies; entire sections of commerce (e.g., the Merchant Marine) are placed under military control. While the nation's industrial capacity in wartime may be basically the same as it is in peacetime, the priorities have to undergo change. Managers do not suddenly become more talented when war is declared, but they are able to reduce a number of conflicts and make better use of resources. Things are made much simpler with only one major customer (i.e., the government) to serve.

Availability of strategic materials and industrial capacity can dictate the time, the place, and even the pace of military action. During World War II, oil was an especially critical resource for Germany; little or none was produced there. Africa and the Middle East became very important; obtaining crude oil for the support of the government plans was worth the extra effort.

In wartime, the government supports and controls both the military and much of the civilian sector, and the usual types of guidelines do not appear to apply. One tendency is to spend whatever is necessary to support the nation at war. When peacetime returns, businesses return to the short leash that requires them to show a profit. In doing so, they must try to balance a wide range of economic variables. There are the common trends (growth, inflation, etc.), the inevitable cycles of ups and downs (recession, recovery), the seasonal variations (the retailers' Christmas cheer), and other patterns of change (interest rates). To these we must also add the need for specific material resources and the training of a labor force unique to each corporation.

Technology (e.g., a breakthrough in weapons development, advantage in product research).   New ideas and technical breakthroughs come from the cooperation of military and business in research. Aside from such well-known examples as the modern computer, atomic energy, space exploration, and telecommunications, there are literally thousands of other offshoots: radar and operations research, methods of pilot training, language classes, emergency medical techniques and trauma centers, all-weather clothing and rations, and numerous other products of military-business research.

One hazard of a rapidly expanding technology is that neither military nor civilian managers see all the possibilities. After World War I, senior officers of the U.S. Army saw little value in the Christie tank, which that was then under development, so the designer began to look elsewhere in hopes of finding a buyer. He found one in Soviet Russia. The U.S.-designed weapon was adopted and later modified to become the T-34 tank, which came back to haunt U.S. commanders in the Korean War. On the civilian side, after World War II there were few U.S. businesses clamoring for the production ideas of W. Edwards Deming. Deming taught in the United States before going to work with the occupation forces in Japan. He inspired their success in improving factory operations.

Today, there are almost daily advances in materials and hardware (robots, computers, etc.), information (data, research results, etc.), knowledge methods (software, statistical and human behavior techniques, etc.), and exciting communication capabilities (videoteleconferencing vs. travel). Still other advances are being evaluated for greater military and civilian use. We are already finding out where robots can be more cost-effective (e.g., no benefits package) than people in a manufacturing environment, how computers are more efficient than human calculators, and when the use of teleconferencing rather than travel by busy managers can save us more time and money.

Competition (e.g., from a variety of enemy forces, from other business practitioners). Sections of the military service are grouped into areas of activity such as the army, the air force, or the navy. These include special subsets such as infantry, armor, or artillery. In business, we have even more specialties. Companies are active in areas of agriculture, manufacturing, and service as well as combinations thereof. Various sections of commerce are land-intensive (farming, ranching), labor-intensive (medicine, food service), capital-intensive (banking, investments), information-intensive (education, research), energy-intensive (metals, transportation), and so on. Each is affected differently by the environmental impacts we have mentioned, which also serves to bring us back to the problem of A working with B from the previous chapter. We can always study each problem as we would study a gemstone we have chosen to set in a ring. We might simplify its description to color, weight, and cut. Unfortunately, this is seldom enough; this simplification may not describe the special diamond that sparkles and reflects with its many facets.

And Other Conditions, Not Seen

Every game-playing contestant tries to anticipate his opponent's next move. This also applies in a business situation. For example, the competitors of one outstanding company apparently assumed that the company's reputation for quality was purchased with research investments so high that the company would soon be forced to increase its selling prices. The competitors were looking at a different side of the diamond. In fact, the company was avoiding expensive research by simply waiting for others to lead the way and then copying what was successful. Their advantage over any company that did the research and development was in cost-cutting and personal service; with these they became a fearsome adversary to anyone else in the field.

Even more embarrassing than being outsmarted is being caught unprepared. To gain the advantage of surprise or to avoid being caught napping, a master player constantly reviews information on the market and every competitor in it. After World War II, the Japanese trading companies became renowned for their study of American markets. Anyone who has reason to doubt this can conduct his own research at the nearest American restaurant. The print on a stainless steel knife or fork may simply read "Japan," but the message is more profound. The Japanese do not use knifes and forks; they use chopsticks, and to undersell Americans, they had to do their homework. Sun Tzu had already said it: "If you know the enemy, and know yourself, you need not fear the result of a hundred battles."

Careful preparation and early information are the best antidotes for surprise. Gaining thorough knowledge of the terrain and keeping a constant eye on the enemy are the best ways for a military commander to avoid surprise. The ultimate objective in battle is to destroy the will of the enemy, but, before this is likely to happen, the commander must first make certain that his own army can survive the other's attack. In business, the rules are much the same. The results may not be measured by dead and wounded, but, if a company is caught by surprise or is outmaneuvered, its chance to succeed is diminished.

Although good planning and information can help to protect a firm or an army from attack, a lack of knowledge or understanding only hastens defeat. Information can also be distorted; this game can be played by both sides. If an opponent is convinced that he knows what we intend to do, we may give him more information that tends to support what he already believes. If he can be led to believe that our progress is less than he expects, he may not try to improve.

"Stonewall" Jackson, during the Civil War, time and again caught his opponents off guard by the simple device of marching faster than they thought was possible. Napoleon had done the same thing many years before him and frequently beat smart generals who had their own fixed ideas on how fast or how far large bodies of troops could move. The best commanders know that the factors of time and space are constant only in the mind of the most self-assured. On the business side, American manufacturers of the 1980s were, time and again, amazed at the speed with which the Japanese could come to market with new products or retool and modify old ones. Experience tables are not set in stone; anything can undergo change.

To avoid unpleasant surprises, it is good to remember two of the most basic military lessons: 1) don't try to guess the enemy's intentions (he can change them at any time), and 2) base your actions on his capabilities (these are not as easy to change). He may try to give you false information on what he intends to do, but the range of his capabilities is open to your analysis.

Another important thing to remember is that we can always learn something from others. When Genghis Khan and his Mongol horsemen first attacked the Chinese, they were slowed down by the fortified cities. The Mongols, however, were quick to adapt; they captured enemy engineers and learned the tricks of their trade. In fact, they learned the lessons so well that Chinese generals, in later battles, were not prepared for the rapidity with which the Khan's troops could reduce the strongest fortress.

The Mongols were not unique. After World War II, Japanese business people used every opportunity to study English and to learn about markets in the United States. Just a few years later, many American businessowners were no better prepared for Japanese competition than the Chinese were for the Khan.

Guess What the Future Might Be

Every military service has experts who scan the world for clues to anything that could trigger an international incident or help their side in a war. Smart businesspeople also keep informed on what the future could bring. Some very intelligent individuals question whether we can discern the future, but there is really no choice— we must try.

Newer methods for predicting the future are always being developed. One popular approach today is the practice of writing scenarios. This is one of the many techniques used by members of the World Future Society, an organization devoted to the study of possible future conditions and factors that influence what those conditions might be. The emphasis is not so much on forecasting as it is on attempts to anticipate a wide range of possibilities. The basic idea is to develop three different sets of conditions: an optimistic view, a pessimistic one, and something in between. The approach is similar in many respects to that of the "estimate of the situation" used for military intelligence and decision analysis. It amounts to 1) listing the courses of action or events that could occur, 2) selecting the most likely conditions among these possibilities, and 3) estimating the impacts or results.

As a civilian example of this approach, let us suppose that a market researcher wishes to study the effect of population increase in a market area or an influx of new people into that market area. If we assume that the study is confined to a region in the southern United States, the sequence might go as follows:

1. A listing of the *possible* situations or events (e.g., the different types of people who could move into the area). This could result in a very long list that could include many types of retired persons, back-to-the-landers, "urban escapees," Mexican workers, anyone wishing to avoid cold weather, and so on. The possibilities are limited only by the imagination of the study participants.

2. A selection of the *most probable* conditions (e.g., new residents). Dependent on the location, one very likely group to move in might be retirees escaping the cold northern winters. Mexican workers from the south could be another such group. For simplicity, we shall limit the discussion to the first one of these.

3. An estimation of the *impact* of one of these groups (e.g., retirees) on the area. With more retired people, the number of households on a fixed income will increase. Those retirees will be less

mobile than the general population and will have fewer children at home. They are more likely to register as voters and, as a group, are not so quick to vote for such items as new highways or costly equipment for schools. On the other hand, they would favor improvements in medical services, initiatives to reduce utility costs, improvements in TV reception, and so on.

With this simplified type of analysis, not every event will be anticipated, but, if a serious effort is made, most major activities or events are likely to be recognizable. The result of such planning is that a wide range of possibilities will be considered, and the evaluation completed in a fairly consistent framework. No attempt is made to forecast every conceivable event, but rather attempts are made to anticipate likely events and then to make plans to address them. We know we cannot be certain about what will happen, but we can often do better planning, just because we have tried. The future is always before us, and we want to deal with what comes. Charles Kettering, General Motors' famous inventor-whiz, is supposed to have once said, "I am very much interested in the future—I expect to spend the rest of my life there."

In this discussion of impacts, especially from the external environment, we have tried to list many factors and to consider them one at a time. While this process is simple and easy to organize, it is never a complete picture of reality. It is only when we think in terms of these things and how they are acting together that we come close to life as we find it. Sometimes we are surprised at how well we can put the pieces together. A simple classroom exercise gives us one illustration. If we take a topographic map of the United States that shows only the natural features (i.e., no roads, buildings, or other human-made objects), we can make a very good guess at where major cities will be. This is because rivers, natural harbors, mountain ranges, and temperate latitudes give us many important clues about where people might congregate and how transportation centers develop. Here we can make good use of available information, but we must also heed a bit of a warning. In the future, we are sure to find changes. The world continues to grow smaller and more interactive; rapidly expanding technologies are a considerable help in dealing with problems affecting environments. An abundance of natural resources may be translated into better technology (e.g., as in Saudi Arabia, Kuwait, etc.), while improved materials or financial assistance (e.g., the Marshall Plan) may speed up needed rebuilding after natural disasters or war.

The competitor, technology, and the future all combine to pose many interesting problems for the military commander or the business chief. Decision-making procedures developed in the military have long been applied to a wide range of business problems and, when combined with computing techniques, are finding still greater use in many areas of free enterprise. One single item, the computer (first built to calculate ballistic firing tables), has already revolutionized every facet of management in every field of endeavor. Unfortunately, it is relatively little used by those at the top of the ladder. We could argue that the judgments required by generals and chief executives exceed the thinking capacity of any electronic brain. Still, there are others who say that this is a weak excuse; that there is great unused computing power standing at the ready today. Physicians and other professionals have developed expert systems programs that serve as ready consultants with independent opinions or diagnostic reviews. If the consultant program developed from the experience of hundreds of professionals agrees with her own opinion, a doctor can feel more confident of her professional skills. In management decision making, the parallel does not yet seem to exist, but managers do use the computer to check information resources and provide mental models of "what if" scenarios that help in decision making.

There is another interesting problem here. As the computer becomes better able to serve in decision making, every senior manager will have access to equally powerful programs. As improved methods are perfected, they will be matched by other programs available to competitors. Fortunately, a solution to this type of standoff has long existed in business practice: the most creative thinker will always lead the pack. Another common solution is also frequently tried, namely, better use of all the human brains that are part of the firm. One of the greatest untapped resources is the mind of the worker. More effective use of workers' minds is one of the challenges for the manager in years ahead.

In 1288 B.C., Ramses II may have been guilty of failing to do his homework—a closer study of the territory—but he reacted vigorously when his column was ambushed at Kadesh. In A.D. 1982, the chairman of Johnson & Johnson reacted almost as promptly when one of his products was ambushed. In that year, Tylenol, a popular drug from the company, was the target of malicious tampering that resulted in several fatalities from poison. In the first few weeks following the deaths, sales of the product were down by almost 90 percent; however, the company quickly began a recall and repackaging effort designed to reduce the likelihood that such a poisoning would happen again. They also issued free coupons for new replacement product. Management skillfully used advertising, news releases, and personal appearances on national networks to explain their corrective actions. To the complete surprise of many observers, in just a few months the company had recovered most of its market. Aggressive action by the chief executive was no doubt a critical factor, but a reputation for trustworthiness and a high degree of familiarity on the part of management with the social environment and the marketplace also helped quite a bit.

— 4 —

Be Ready to Deal with the Worst

There was no doubt that the king was in trouble; he and his whole country were surrounded by enemy armies. Things were very gloomy indeed, except for one thing—Frederick II knew exactly where he was weak, yet he was confident of his strengths. He had felt this confidence since he had won a series of battles as a young king. In fact, his boldness became a concern to other heads of state—and brought on consensus that the upstart German ruler would have to be put in his place. Thus, in 1756, Prussia found it-self facing the field armies of Austria, France, Russia, and Sweden at the onset of the Seven Years' War. The combined population of the countries opposing him was on the order of 100 million people, but Frederick could only count about five million people in Prussia. The odds did not appear to faze him. His army was already one of the best in Europe, and he was its able commander.

As the buildup in fighting progressed, the allies could not seem to get their project together. Frederick was able to keep their armies off balance and confronted each one in turn. The years of warfare continued, but the basic conditions did not change. Eventually a truce was arranged with no major changes in territory or demands for tribute or reparations. Boundaries remained much as they had been before, but there was one important difference—the other countries were forced to accept the presence of Prussia as a major power on the continent. In time, the unconventional monarch would become known as Frederick the Great, and cited as one of the "great captains" in Western military history. From his time onward, Prussia's influence in Europe would continue to grow (even to the present day).

The Critical Job at the Top

Many observers who focus on the chief executives see them as public figures who reflect the organization. Those on the outside recognize them as the people in charge and look to these movers and shakers as the people who get things done.

Thus, it is easy to see that one of the most important resources of any organization is the person at the top of the chart. The chief is in the best place to make important decisions; he or she is in a position to see the greatest number of problem areas and often has the longest reach into the future.

The chief's position is unusual in still another way; it is the loneliest place on earth. Though constantly meeting with people, too often they are like total strangers when outside the corporate world; there are very few, if any, people with whom they can share their true feelings. They live in a world where whatever is said will be repeated, restated in a dozen different ways, some of which will not be intended. As a result, they must always be conscious of any ideas they convey to others and how those ideas can color recipients' views. When they ask for advice or information, they know the reply will seldom be free from bias or given without the prospect of gain. Unless they make an effort to avoid it, they will soon be tended by sycophants, exposed to oceans of good news, and shielded from all that is bad.

Not only must chief executives study the behavior of others, they must also stand aside and look at their own performance. In the ideal situation, they would do this with clear objectivity, as if through the eyes of others.

Frederick understood all this quite well. Among other requirements for his generals, he looked for acting ability. He expected the commander to convince his troops that they knew exactly what the commander was planning while the commander was concealing his actual intentions. A more important reason for requiring acting ability, however, was to enable commanders to project an aura of certainty; thus, subordinates would be convinced that whatever actions were being planned would certainly lead to success. It is well-known that any commander's show of confidence in the face of danger and doubtful circumstance can set the mood for an operation; the leader's conspicuous conduct becomes the critical standard by which behavior is judged.

When changes are made in expected actions or previously stated priorities, those changes get closer attention and then are often widely copied (and sometimes widely criticized). This even applies to routine management actions. A simple visit to Plant A or Plant B may set in motion a whole chain of new events and speculation totally unknown to the senior manager and the staff. For example, when the chief executive visits Plant A three times and goes to Plant B only once, there is a sudden development of greater interest in what is going on at Plant A or questions are raised about why Plant B is ignored. Actually, Plant B may be making excellent progress or may just need a little more time in a particular area. Of course, it may be that Plant A is the headquarters' favorite. For whatever reason, any area or activity in which the chief shows undue interest will usually draw added attention, resulting in extra effort. The conventional wisdom has always been that "the troops do well what the commander inspects." It should also be noted that the personality of a chief executive often adds to an already forceful advertisement of what actions should be.

In warfare, each of the contending sides makes an effort to obtain data on the opposite chief. If a leader has ever shown signs of bias or indecision, one can be sure that a record has been made. If he is the best swordsman or pistol shot, his prowess will be widely known. In fact, the intelligence section of every major headquarters has long kept an "Order of Battle" on units they are likely to meet. It contains information on the unit's training and equipment status, a record of its battle experience, and details on who the commanders are or have been. In business, the problem of collecting this information is actually much easier; a city library will often have considerable material on the history and current status of numerous public firms, even including data on most of the key executives. Unfortunately, much of the usual data (age, education, etc.) tells us very little about what the chief executive can do. Human behavior is one of the most complex of subjects, and it is no great surprise that we find so many different personalities in the various leaders of business or war. If one chief is unseemingly rash, another is too cautious or too slow. If one is logical and favors good order, another one is creative and ready to try new things. Some executives are more liberal in their viewpoint while others are very conservative. One manager may favor a centralized form of decision making; another wants multiple views. Then there are those who favor letting subordinates decide. Some feel they must focus on getting the work out and that workers should do as they are told. An equal number will argue that people are number one; that there are more important things than work that is finished on time. One good manager is careful to plan ahead; another one, also effective, is certain that the future is unknowable, and that planning is wasting one's time. What soon becomes apparent is that if we rated the characteristics just mentioned and took them as possibilities, the number of combinations in personality types would be greater than we could examine.

It is quite easy to find a paradox in the demands we place on the chief. While there are good reasons to emphasize individual freedoms and the human side of the enterprise, we are sometimes in the position of wanting the manager to keep people happy while he or she makes sure that unpleasant work gets done. We often assume that the manager will insure that the workers' voices, however many, have a chance to be heard. People should be allowed, and even encouraged, to state an opinion; these contribute to new ideas and help toward better morale. Still, there are other times when it is very important that statements of policy and orders that are set at the top be published and carried out.

There are things that require close attention in certain situations; at other times they are safely ignored. However, in practically every circumstance, there are a few things that must be given priority; they are different from anything else. Frederick put great emphasis on the few items he thought to be critical. Generals were advised to "sacrifice the bagatelle and pursue the essential. The essential is to be found where the big bodies of the enemy are." He held that "petty geniuses attempt to hold everything; wise men hold fast to the most important resort. They parry great blows and scorn little accidents." Those comments were also a reflection of the views of another famous general, Maurice de Saxe, whom Frederick greatly admired. More than 100 years later, the same ideas would surface again in the words of an Italian economist and sociologist named Vilfredo Pareto. Today, Pareto's "80-20" rule is usually stated in the form that 80 percent of a list of items are relatively unimportant; the remaining 20 percent are the critical few. We often find that 80 percent of the value of an inventory is in 20 percent of the items, or that 80 percent of the sales of a firm come from 20 percent of its customers. In combat, Pareto's rule iterates the observation that a few hills and road nets may be far more important than anything else in the zone.

In the case of the chief executive, it is not a matter of 80 and 20; the test is a sample of one. The importance of this single individual is quite dramatically shown when a country's leader—the president, the king, or whatever—is replaced. With the arrival of a new head of state, a different mental atmosphere often comes into being, and a marked change in attitude is seen in the people themselves. A new leader can bring new feelings of hope and confidence, a conviction that problems will really be solved; where before, there seemed only failures and the prospect of further decline. The future is somehow brighter, and prospects for the present improve. All this may seem to be so, even while the actual conditions are not much different from before. In fact, when a new president takes office in the United States, only a small number of new people come with him. Hundreds of thousands of bureaucrats do not move—they stay in their jobs as before. The change that occurs is in the attitude that the new chief executive and a very small group at the top bring into office.

Intangible Types of Resources

A chief executive is the most important resource for a firm, but there are also many others. Some are much more mental than physical.

The small group (the board of directors) that oversees the senior manager can be an important reservoir of past experiences for guiding the organization. In the military, the next higher headquarters is usually headed by older and more senior officers with staffs long tested. In business, members of the board are often chosen for past accomplishments and records of time-tested judgment. These agencies commonly participate in allocations of tangible resources, but they also perform this role in areas involving intangibles (e.g., the hiring of senior executives).

From groups in the external environment come knowledge and other resources. The military commander seeks information on the enemy and studies the physical features of the ground itself. The business executive wants information on competitors while spending much time and effort in finding potential customers. Incidentally, this is not much different from the goal of the military commander who tries to sway civilians away from supporting the enemy.

Inside the organization, interest groups at the troop or employee level provide a critical resource. Here reside the many skills and motivations that also determine success, and it is here where the physical effort must be made. Without that physical effort there is no progress.

A resource that cannot be easily sorted out, but can never be overrated, is the body of common practices and know-how involving operations. This is a unique pattern of policies, rules, and procedures that improve performance. When this body of practices is combined with the overall skills of coordination and leadership, very powerful resources result. Related to this is still another intangible: a structure of the helping elements that support the common effort. One of these elements at the senior level is the concept of general staff.

The General Management Staff

There are many things a chief executive can only do in person; conversely, other tasks can be delegated to subordinates. The military commander must often travel to higher headquarters and give his personal views on the situation. At headquarters, orders for action can be given to him in person as well. The business chief executive is obliged to appear at meetings of the company's board where he can speak for himself. Many of the other actions can be delegated to his representatives.

In a large organization, there are basically three levels of personnel. Starting from the top, they are 1) the senior command or executives, 2) the staff or supporting agencies, and 3) the operating divisions. The highest level (e.g., the Commanding General of Southeastern Command, the Chief Executive of Motorola) is responsible for every aspect of the organization, its structure and its function, its resources, and its success in reaching its objectives. Obviously, no single person can handle the job alone; a number of different assistants are needed. At the upper levels, we find these described with such titles as the Vice President of Administration, the General Staff for Administration and Logistics, and so on.

Some form of staff agency has been performing this service role longer than history records. Even in the biblical days of the shepherds, a rod was the instrument of action or punishment, while the staff was one of support. The staff still continues a support role. While Frederick and Napoleon often made battle plans by themselves and personally guided the action, they still had need for staffs. Some of the activities performed by a few trusted aides were simply extensions of the master's head and his hands—creative thinking by the helpers was infrequently required or even sought.

Today, a chain of command continues to act as the channel of information for action, but a staff can still support operations with additional activities, such as forecasting and general planning, specific task supervision, detailed coordination, and assisting in general control.

After Frederick, the Prussian army began formal programs designed to prepare selected officers to serve on the general's staff. Basically, they were trained to study, plan, advise on, and coordinate major actions as required by the chief executive. By the time of the Franco-Prussian War in 1870, the concept of a general staff was already highly developed as an agency of the high command. It was separate from the various arms of the service (e.g., Infantry, Armor, Artillery, etc.), and the "general" purpose was to support the activities of all elements of the command. In World War II, and in the following years, the German general staff performed functions that have continued to be fairly typical today. The two major areas of activity identified by the German staff were 1) intelligence/operations and 2) administration/logistics. One does not have to look far to find parallels in areas of business activity called plans/operations and administration/logistics in practically all modern firms.

In the U.S. Army, the General Staff Corps continues in much the same tradition as that developed by the German army, but there are some significant differences. In the German view, the general staff shares responsibility along with the commander, whereas in the United States' view, the commander has total responsibility. The General Staff Corps in this country answers only to the commander, even though their actions are designed to support all elements of the command. Aside from philosophic differences on how responsibility should be shared, the work of the general staff in Germany and the United States is similar in many regards. In both cases it serves to collect information, study problems, recommend actions, prepare plans and orders, transmit instructions, and improve coordination.

In the business practices of both Germany and the United States, there are many similarities to practices in the military forces. In

Germany, for example, it is common to find a sharing of responsibility among two or three senior executives at the highest decision-making level. This is somewhat in contrast to the practice in the United States, where the tradition has been to maintain a single chief executive. A parallel to the collegial system found in Germany does exist in the form of the plural executive (e.g., Office of President), but, when this structure is used in American organizations, the final responsibility is still likely to fall on a single chief executive, viewed more as a "first among equals." In times of trouble, he may be the first to be fired, as many who have endured this experience can testify.

The concept of a general staff is apparent in the organizational structure of many firms. For example, the General Electric company chart of the early 1970s shows a corporate executive staff with sections for planning development (plans/operations?), business environment (intelligence?), production and financial resources (logistics?), and a section for the administrative staff. As in the military situation, these are general management functions concerned with common problems that are very broad in scope.

There are other military and business staff sections that reflect more specialized roles. In a military organization, they include sections for legal affairs, the chaplain, civilian activities, and the like. These officers are experts in a particular area but may also serve as the senior commanders of units of specialized troops (e.g., engineer battalions, quartermaster, etc.). In spite of what could be a confusion of titles (e.g., the same individual being the division engineer, commanding officer 1st Engineers, etc.), there is usually no great problem, perhaps because the system has developed from many years of practice. Actually, such overlaps in roles do not present a difficulty, even in civilian practice, where managers may be required to perform two or more types of duties (e.g., on different committees, in temporary matrix structures, special task organizations, etc.) at the same place and time.

Specialized staff positions are also evident in many business enterprises. An organizational chart for General Electric shows sections for a general counsel, public relations, facilities service, and other sections that are quite similar to military staff positions (e.g., legal affairs, civilian activities, engineer, quartermaster, etc.). In fact, the army adjutant on parade, while appearing quite formal in dress and demeanor as he announces the daily orders, is not significantly different in principle from the corporate secretary, performing a similar duty, though with fewer brass buttons and less show.

Teamwork and the Actions Up Front

Activity on the "firing line" of either an army or a corporation is likely to be very physical, while activity that starts at the top is mental. The senior manager first develops a concept, then orients the organization on whatever is to be done, and finally allocates resources to do the job. In the army, a commander, with his staff, develops a general concept of the operation, then the staff and lower commanders elaborate the concept with more details. While this seems simple enough, there is a need for coordination of activities in different levels and zones to improve the chance of success (passing through adjacent units, commanders and staff visits, and establishment of definite contact).

Simply stated, the middle- and lower-level commanders are assigned specific objectives and given a share of resources to be used in completing their part of the task. Such means will include not only personnel and equipment but also other types of support that are not so easily seen (e.g., updated enemy information, guidance on the control of lateral space, allocation of time available, etc.). The lower-level army commander is usually assigned a section of ground, a zone of operation, where his part of the action takes place. This area is marked at the far end by a general objective, and at the near end by a starting line with initial spreads of resources. Simplified, the lines at the start and finish, along with the boundaries on the right and left, form a box of the operation, inside which the unit commander can study and plan local actions. To coordinate with other units, he is given a definite starting time and asked to report on his progress. In sum, the top commander assigns objectives and allocates resources, whereas subordinates provide the action.

Instead of a zone for combat, the manager in a business situation could have a market area, but the concept is almost the same. The area, or zone of action (the market), may still be a type of box. At one end is the objective, at the other end are typical resources. The right and left boundaries may consist of restrictions in space (an assigned geographical area) or a set of monetary restraints (the amount of money that can be committed without having prior approval). Military and business parallels are sometimes not easily seen, but the idea of objectives and the resources to reach them is basic to either type of plan.

In a combat order, the coordination between units must be stated very clearly (e.g., responsibility for maintaining contact to be from the right unit to the left unit, etc.), and the commanding general may set landmarks or specifically labeled checkpoints (along a straight line from the initial point to the final objective) for reporting. The expected time (e.g., D-Day+4, or 1 March 1995) for reaching the final objective is cited for purposes of coordination. Business organizations do not seem to give such detailed attention to the coordination problem, but this can be good or bad. While too much coordination can be restrictive, too little may be expensive, especially if the same wheel is reinvented in every division or project.

Operations in combat can never be judged or analyzed from only one single aspect. Progress may be affected by a number of unfriendly actions in the adjacent combat area, on the ground, in the air, or even out on the sea. Air force or navy support may vary from direct intervention in the combat area, where ground troops can see the results, to actions in distant locations, where the final effects may not be evident for months or sometimes even for years. The destruction of a ball bearing plant does not help an infantry soldier to take his immediate objective, but it can reduce the number of weapons he will have to face in the future. In business, these long-range impacts are more likely to be the result of research programs of the firm or of the efforts of an industry agency (e.g., a lobby organized to improve government regulations or the balance of trade).

Look Forward, Look Back, Look Up, and Look Out

In a military situation, a commander may have to estimate the enemy strength from a look at positions they hold and the types of weapons employed. He may have to guess about the impact of enemy movements with very limited information on the size and direction of convoys. An estimate of enemy capability based on training and morale would be helpful but may be hard to obtain. An experienced military observer can make a working estimate of a unit's effectiveness if he knows a bit of its history; he can do a far better job if he knows the stage of its training, the experience of its commander, and condition of its arms and equipment. He knows that the years of service and tradition will have an impact on the esprit and morale of the soldiers. It is with these and other crude indications of the enemy situation and knowledge of his own units that a commander must judge what to do.

The business chief executive also studies the environment for any new threats or opportunities. When she looks inside the organization, the watchwords are *weakness* and *strength*. She may have an informal list of key factors, but knows that she must still make a judgment call. As in the military situation, the final problem is, in almost every case, that of trying to evaluate one's own strengths or weaknesses with incomplete information and the hazards of personal bias.

Some methods for judging the competition can be helpful in judging oneself. One approach that was mentioned earlier is to start with a general overview, then find the critical factors and relationships, and move from there to the details. For a somewhat different perspective, on occasion it may be of value to think backward through this sequence. Such an approach is suggested in the following listing.

1. First, visualize the mission or project in general terms. Start with the resources and actions necessary for reaching the key objectives, then walk through the plan intended to accomplish the

objectives. One of the biggest problems is to determine what information will be needed to accomplish each step. Another problem is to find out what the pitfalls might be. Then you must visualize how all the steps will fit together.

2. Next, examine the objectives already gained, and think backward through the steps that achieved them. This back-step way of thinking may seem a bit unusual at first, but it is really no different from the process of going forward. The problem is not in thinking backward; it is when we try to take action. For a quick exercise in this, just think of the alphabet as running from Z to A, then take a pencil and write it. Better go back to thinking. In business, backward logic would have us start with the market or customer (sales), then step backward to production or service (costs). While reviewing the steps in this manner, we can sometimes see better ways to coordinate our actions in both directions. A different perspective on areas and activities (e.g., sales vs. inventories) combined with an examination of the many resources available (money and material, labor and skills) provides a useful means of reviewing multiple trends from the past and helps guide us into the future.

It is easy to get bogged down in details and sometimes hard to get out. While a new perspective can help, the basic question still remains: What is important? A work group may have the managers and operator skills but still lack other resources (e.g., modern tools) for doing a good job. A manufacturing division may be confident that its product quality is first-rate and that it has no further need to study competitors. A company may have a good reputation today but have little concern for the future. A general management analysis cannot be used to make the final judgment until it includes the weight of many factors and an examination of those factors' interaction (How could the twenty A's affect the forty B's, and what could the outcome be?).

Still, there are some who would ask if it is really better to start at the top (even with the biggest picture), or whether it is better to start at the bottom with a greater knowledge of the details. The answer we offer here is *both*. The "big picture" provides a basic framework, a format for placing key facts, and a very early guess at the solution to the puzzle. But in everyday situations, only a limited number of key elements will be likely to be known or recognized. In the final analysis, the study must both start and end with a look at the chief executive and a balanced view of the world.

Always an Eye on the Chief

A few years ago, anyone would know that Henry Ford was the critical element at Ford Motor Company, as were the Watsons at IBM, and David Sarnoff at RCA. Today, we can still recognize that a major factor in an organization is the manager at the top. The chief is the focus of a thousand eyes, and of pressures from inside and out.

Actually, these pressures come from three bases of concentration, each one an arrow aimed in a different direction. For the organization, they are groups of diverse shareholders or contributors whose efforts must be acknowledged.

If sketched on a piece of paper, the first arrow could be represented as coming from the left and outside with the aim to the right. It would represent the many impacts from an external environment and the public's view of the firm. Here are all of the outside observers that study the chief executive; these include a wide range of interests. In the military, they might be anything from a collection of enemy spies to groups of friendly civilians. For a business, they could be anything from happy and unhappy customers to potential investors and analysts who are watching the company's stocks and bonds.

A second arrow could be shown hanging like a vertical spearpoint over the head of the chief. The aim this time is downward; its target is never in doubt. It comes from different agencies that oversee the firm; especially those charged with general guidance or that help the firm in reaching its goals. In the military, this would be the next-higher headquarters; for a business, it is sometimes a government agency, but in most cases it is the board of directors. In effect, they have a seat at a giant magnifying glass for the purpose of examining the chief.

The third arrow can be represented as having a base on the ground with its point aimed upward. Its point is the concentrated attention of all the groups that are inside the firm. The chief draws their eyes to the top, is constantly "on stage," and has many curious observers.

The points of concern of these three interest groups can also be used to identify three major types of objectives that apply to any large organization. The job of the senior manager is to balance the various groups' objectives and to integrate resources to reach them. This number of interest groups is a challenge to any leader, even the very best.

In response to the group of interests external to the enterprise, the military commander has a simple basic objective: destroy the enemy's will to fight at the minimum cost to his own resources. For a business executive it appears to be much the same: seek to reduce the competitor's hope of gaining more market share while persuading customers that the executive's company provides a quality product at fair cost. In either case, the ideal is to reach important objectives with the minimum cost in resources.

The normal oversight groups in the military (higher headquarters) expect that the commander will first ensure that all units will survive as a fighting unit, then complete the overall mission that includes the stated objectives. In a business situation, the oversight group (the board of directors) looks for the chief executive to minimize overall risk, then works to improve the value of the firm through profit and market achievements.

The groups inside a military organization expect the senior commander to improve work conditions, when possible, and they expect there to be reasonable pay and benefits. Though circumstances obviously differ, the employee groups in a business have almost the same objectives: reasonable working conditions and competitive pay, including a range of benefits.

Thus, from the overall perspective, a chief executive may be described as a person concerned with reaching three general objectives: survival of the organization, service to the groups of contributors, and growth in capability to meet and solve future problems. These objectives recapitulate the keystones of management with which we began: using resources to reach objectives while building for greater challenge.

It is important to mention that, even while working to accomplish the firm's major objectives and to balance the demands of many different interest groups, the chief is also involved with a host of related problems. One is the task of satisfying the needs of a group of people while being aware of the interests of each individual. Another, equally critical task is to accept the changing requirements in his or her own job as well as personal responsibility for errors in judgment. The chief is responsible, as we have said many times, for everything the organization does or fails to do. Like Damocles in olden times, there is, above the head of the chief, a sword that is held by a single thread.

During the Seven Years' War, the objective of Frederick the Great was not in conquering Europe—he lacked resources to do so. Instead, he used what he had to survive and to neutralize the efforts of larger armies that aimed to destroy him. He also served the needs of his country, both outside and inside the army. With his careful analysis of the situation and with his available strengths, he was an important instrument in the drawing of the political map of Europe.

In the early 1980s, the U.S. computer industry was dominated by large and experienced competitors expecting to hold or expand their respective market shares. There were such giants as Texas Instruments, Tandy, and IBM, the biggest computer company of all. One new and much smaller company had a problem similar to that faced by Frederick and his countrymen earlier. The managers of this company chose to follow the path of Prussia: they took note of their greatest strengths and tried to play down their weaknesses. They did not compete in every market; their product was a small computer, designed for ease of use and presented at lower cost. In spite of the giants that faced them, they gained begrudging respect from the best of their kind in the market. Like Frederick and Prussia before them, Steve Jobs and Apple Computer survived their awesome rivals and came to be widely recognized as a major power in the market.

— 5 —

Assign Objectives,
Not Actions

At the coronation ceremony some months before, he had taken the crown from the hands of the pope and placed it on his own head. There was no question that he was Emperor of the French. Recently, he had been preparing for another of his favorite projects: an invasion across the English Channel. It did not matter that experts viewed the operation as impossible, given the physical obstacles and the power of the British navy. Being easily discouraged was not one of Napoleon Bonaparte's most obvious characteristics. It was 1805, and he was the dominant power on the continent—all from a knowledge of strategy.

What Clausewitz and Jomini Saw

To students of warfare, Napoleon was one of the most outstanding commanders in history. It is said that he fought more battles than Hannibal, Alexander, and Julius Caesar combined. He has been called the greatest military strategist of the Western world, and a study of his campaigns is basic to an understanding of the concept of strategy as we describe it today.

Many authors have given their opinions on Napoleon's approach to warfare and have offered various possible reasons for the French army's success. Two of the most important observers came from outside of France. One of these was Prussian, the other was Swiss. Karl von Clausewitz is still widely known for his treatise *On War*, but few people would recognize the name Antoine Henri Jomini or his book, *Summary of the Art of War*, though he served on Napoleon's staff and studied him in close detail. Jomini's writings, when compared to the sometimes more difficult observations of Clausewitz, are fairly straightforward in their impressions and often easier to follow. However, in spite of any differences in analysis or writing style, both came to the same conclusion: military operations are complex in nature, but do involve some fundamental principles that cannot be safely ignored.

Strategy, as we already know, is broad in its scope and very diverse in its content. In a military situation, it encompasses a large geographical region, also known as the theater of operations. This theater can include a part of a country, an entire country, or even a group of several countries. The range of locations and activities is such that all aspects of this area can be visualized only in the mind—it is simply not possible to observe each of the separate elements individually at one time. A general cannot, in person, lead every one of his troops into battle, just as the chief executive of a business of any size cannot personally supervise each of the operating locations or service activities for which he is held responsible. It was probably for this reason that Jomini described strategy as the art of making war on a map, where symbols could be used to indicate units and to emphasize features of the land.

In land warfare, the focus is very much on the ground form and the physical characteristics of the area. In business, we use the more abstract concept of the "market." Jomini would probably argue that strategy, for the business chief executive, is the art of conceptualizing a rather extensive market. As in the case of the military situation, this also assumes the use of maps, many kinds of visual aids, and verbal and written reports.

In an early chapter of *Summary of the Art of War*, Jomini points out that strategy takes in a number of separate elements within a unified scheme. Its study thus involves many different elements examined first individually, then in interaction, and finally, as a whole. In the section that follows, we shall draw attention to some of the critical factors he mentions. We have also added remarks, in parentheses, that may help in reviewing his comments. The paragraph numbers are from notes in *Summary of the Art of War*.

Based on Jomini's analysis of Napoleon's campaigns, some basic components of strategy are as follows:

1. Selection of a theater of operation. (The strategist must first decide where the action will take place. For an army, this is the area it chooses to attack or defend; it is the territory "upon which the parties may assail each other." Presumably, it is a region well suited to the strategist's intentions, and a careful analysis of the region in which an effort is made is required. For a business, that region is the market in which the business will compete, and that region requires an intensive study, no less than does a theater of operation in war.)

2. Determination of decisive points and the overall direction for operations. (The "decisive point" in commerce may be somewhat more abstract. It could be a time that is chosen for the introduction of a new product or the place in which the business enters a market. It might even be the choice of the type of market to enter, or a response to a competitor's action. For Montgomery Ward vs. Sears, the decisive point was the anticipated economic environment that followed World War II. For the Ford Motor Company in the 1920s, it was style and model change in automobiles. For IBM in the 1980s, it was probably the microcomputer. The "direction for operations" may be described as "forward" for an increase in activity, "backward" for a withdrawal or reduction in scope, or "holding" for maintaining or improving one's position.)

3. Selection and establishment of a base and of a zone of operations. (This base is the logistical base, a concept equally valid in business or war. As stated before, the first priority must be given to resources and actions that will ensure survival. Expensive lessons have been learned when this has been taken too lightly. Napoleon himself, in 1812, was forced to retreat from Moscow because his troop strength was too low for effective operations. In

business, if money is not available to support the growth that is planned, if provisions are not made to support the growth that is planned, or if inventories are not available to meet orders, customers will go to vendors who appear to be better prepared.)

4. Selection of the objective point. (A statement of the overall purpose of the mission and guidance is always the best place to start for considering the detailed objectives. The first objective to be examined must always be survival. Analysis of the problem of meeting the needs of many important contributors such as customers, workers, and investors is needed. In a combat zone, objectives are usually stated with reference to accessible and clearly defined terrain features; business textbooks always stress the need for clear and attainable goals.)

A different kind of objective is important when an organization concentrates on improvement and growth. An army constantly updates its training plans; business managers strive to improve efficiency. In addition, there is ever a need to remind ourselves that the actions and the objectives are in constant interaction. Customers are always looking for better prices, and this may be in conflict with the workers' equally constant demand for higher wages or the investors' perception of an ongoing right to dividends. Of course, government, at every level, continues its own search for contributions and ways to obtain more money.

Elements 5 through 8 in Jomini's book are not presented here; they seem only to elaborate on the others already discussed. There is, however, one other item that deserves attention.

9. The march of armies or maneuvers. (An element of strategy that includes the movement and appropriate positioning of resources before the fighting begins is addressed here. Though this activity may take place at some distance from the battlefield, its importance cannot be overestimated. Napoleon was acutely aware of the need for and the placement of resources before beginning an engagement. His usual practice was to move his major units, each by a different route, to a forward assembly area from which they would deploy for combat. Because of the great amount of time they would spend marching, his soldiers sometimes said they

"fought the wars with their feet." In business, an effort to gain the best initial position in a market may be different from such an effort in war, but the principle is still much the same. Branch offices are opened, new salespeople are trained and assigned, and inventories are established at the best possible locations for responding to future contingencies. All this must take place before the real action occurs.)

Long-range preparation and maneuver, along with proper positioning, are vital both to military strategy and to corporate strategy. By comparison, in tactics, the action is short-term and brief. A closer look at strategy and tactics may help to clarify the differences between them.

In strategy, as we already know, the theater of operations is the whole, the battlefield is only a part. All or most of the action cannot be seen by one observer; it is often just seen as a series of marks on a map. The picture presented here is made up of the larger elements of an organization in extended spaces and time. On the other hand, tactics is oriented toward units on the battlefield, to a more limited range of the action.

Like the word *strategy*, the term *tactics* comes from another Greek word, *taktika*. It was used to describe the order or arrangement of troops as they stood ready for battle. There is no shortage of detail; the fighters stand face to face. Strategy, in many respects, has more the aspect of gaming and intellect (e.g., aircraft commanders may simply report the percentage of the target that was covered; there is no name list of casualties). Tactics, on the other hand, involves a very personal and emotional experience; the attackers cry out as they rush forward, the defenders panic and run. Strategy determines what markets to enter; tactics defines how to serve the customer.

Almost a Bloodless Gunfight

In 1805, Napoleon dominated Europe, but not everyone was willing to kowtow to him. In southern Europe, the Austrian military corps and their Italian counterparts saw the action on the beaches of northern France as a diversion and an opportunity to catch the Corsican by surprise. They set about to lure him into a situation where he could be put at a disadvantage and, presumably, then defeated. They expected to regain the territory previously lost to him and perhaps even extend their control to other areas. Following this general approach, they developed a plan whereby a joint Austrian-Italian task force would take the offensive in Italy, and, at the same time, a separate Austrian army would establish a defensive position in southern Germany. Russia had also agreed to support the Austrian plan. According to the allies' expectations, the French, finding the allies already superior in two places, would be forced to divide their army. As a consequence of all this, by September, the Austrian army was at the border of southern Germany, ready to go into action.

Archduke Ferdinand was in titular command of the Austrian army; but Emperor Francis was the supreme commander, and he chose to appoint General Karl Mack von Leiberich as his senior military advisor. On his arrival on the frontier, Mack gave orders for the army to advance into Bavaria. Ferdinand, who had planned to wait until the Russians were in a better position, ordered the movement to halt. The emperor decided in favor of Mack, and the Austrians continued on to take up their positions in Germany. The lack of unified effort displayed by the three leaders so early in the campaign could easily be viewed as an omen of future difficulty in cooperation. There is reputed to be an old Chinese saying, "If three would agree, they could turn mud into gold." The allies would need all the coin they could get.

Napoleon was soon made aware of the Austrian movements and quickly understood their intent. He decided that his plans for the invasion would have to wait and began his own move toward the Rhine. A few of the forward units were directed to the Black Forest region, where they began a series of actions to probe the Austrian positions. This, of course, the allies had expected and was in accord with their plan. Unknown to the Austrian leaders, however, large elements of Napoleon's army were moving on to the east in what was to be a wide turning movement at the right (north) flank of the Austrian positions. When this maneuver was completed, the mass of the French army would be in a position to create a threat to the opposition's key supply lines, thus putting the Austrian effort at risk. In one coordinated movement, Napoleon had not only set out to confound the allies' plans, but to rearrange the battle positions, and ensure the Austrians' defeat.

The outlines of Napoleon's maneuver can be seen in Figure 5.1.

The figure attempts to reduce the campaign at Ulm to three basic components of strategy: resources (X), actions (Y), and objectives (Z).

French reconnaissance units engaged the forward elements of General Mack's army, which was already in defensive positions. This led the Austrians to believe that the French units were testing

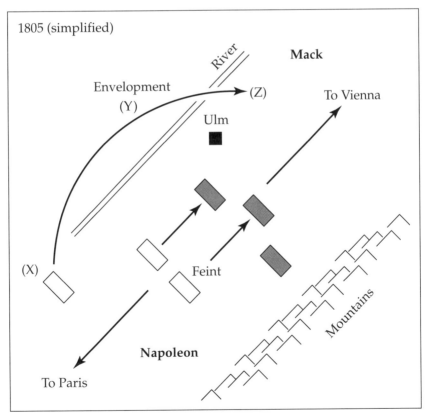

Figure 5.1 Napoleon's Campaign at Ulm

their strength and would soon launch a frontal attack. Instead, the major units of the French army were being deployed to positions north of the Danube River where they could focus on the right flank of the Austrian positions. Napoleon's first objective was to concentrate his forces at Ulm. From there he could threaten or disrupt the communications and supply lines to the rear and force the Austrian army to turn right and fight in a totally different direction. Mack was not prepared for this eventuality. When Napoleon was able to concentrate his forces, the defeat of the Austrian army was only a matter of time. By placing his units in positions that took the most advantage of the terrain, Bonaparte had effectively reduced by one-half the size of the enemy force that could engage him (i.e., only Mack's northern sector could promptly respond to attacks). At the same time, the French stood to cut off Austrian supplies and reinforcements and block any aid from the Russians. In fact, before the Austrians knew it had started, the campaign at Ulm was over.

Strategy and CENCO, S.A.

Move forward now to the 1980s. The place is still Western Europe, but imagine a business scenario. A key player at this time is a French company with many years in the mainframe computer business. In 1985, CENCO, S.A., was about to expand its research and development efforts into wider applications for mainframes and supercomputers. It planned to go into active competition with Wave Development, a British company already known as a leader in very large computers.

While CENCO was studying the problem of how best to compete with Wave, it also learned that some of its own competitors were increasing their market activities. Eagle Computers, an Austrian manufacturer, held a modest share of the market in middle-sized computers, known as "minicomputers," and was negotiating a joint venture with Appian Data, an Italian computer firm. It seemed that their joint intent was to offer a "supermini" that would compete with the lower end of the mainframe market now dominated by CENCO. Also rumored to be participating in this venture was URSA, an older technology company with a base in Eastern Europe.

The plan appeared to have many parts. Initially, Eagle would test the market in southern Germany with the "super minicomputer." CENCO was expected to respond to this new competition, but the feeling was that any significant action could be more than matched by the Eagle-Appian-URSA team. In fact, the trio seemed to believe that the project would soon establish their reputation as new leaders in the mainframe market.

When the news of the Eagle-Appian-URSA project became more widely known, the CENCO management team, as expected, felt compelled to respond to the threat. Its divisions were instructed to devote extra efforts to the lower end of the market. This action was designed to reduce any losses in regular mainframe customers.

Eagle and its partners were expecting such a move by CENCO; it was all a part of their plan. Unfortunately for them, however, there were other things that had not been so clearly foreseen. CENCO had decided to go even further and implement an aggressive but secret research program to expand its own market share. Accordingly, they allocated more resources to a wide range of developmental activities (e.g., projects to improve product designs, to convert plant equipment, to retrain personnel, etc.) that would result in the best and most flexible line of small computers that could be made with existing technology. These "supermicros" would be very powerful personal computers capable of competing with minicomputers in the same market that Eagle thought the allies controlled. CENCO had not been active in this area before, and such an entry was not expected in response to the joint-venture plan. Even less foreseen was still another burst of CENCO activity, which was a plan to include the most advanced components into a cost-effective small computer suitable for direct competition with the dominant Eagle brand line. The CENCO projects were undertaken with the tightest security measures and no public speculation was acknowledged.

By the middle of 1985, CENCO was engaged in the following both open and secret activities:

1. A limited number of modified CENCO computers were introduced to compete with established Eagle minicomputers to the service and industrial markets. (Feint.)

2. High priority had been given to producing a new supermicrocomputer for shipping late in the year. This product would be in direct competition with computers now being offered by the Eagle-URSA combine. (Main effort.)

By late 1985, Eagle was experiencing problems with its superminicomputer (the mainframe competitor). Having neither the experience nor the technical resources of CENCO, Eagle was not yet in good enough condition to push for maximum sales. CENCO, on the other hand, had been able to achieve significant cost savings and was confident that it could go for a price lower than that of the standard Eagle computers. The company had so intensified its research and production efforts that it now had a significant inventory of the new supermicros; it was ready for a formal announcement of the existence of the supermicros and the first show of advertising and sales.

Eagle's top managers were caught completely off guard by the introduction of the new CENCO supermicrocomputer. They were especially dumbfounded by its ability to perform functions previously thought limited to larger computers. This revelation, along with CENCO's well-known reputation for service after the sale, and the cost savings represented by the new computer produced an overwhelming effect on Eagle computer sales. Eagle management made haste to reappraise the partnership option, but the hour was already late. Eagle was forced to make a multi-million dollar write-off on inventory that was now obsolete; company profits rapidly sank; and the stock prices went toward the bottom. Efforts to reorganize were ineffective, and there were questions whether they could continue as a going concern. URSA did not offer much help. In the end, it was clear that Eagle was almost approaching collapse and that CENCO had found a new market. To no one's surprise, the questions were already being raised about fair trade practices (CENCO's developmental activities had certainly been unexpected), but these were met by equally strident counterclaims that the results were due to the excellence of CENCO management. Whatever the criteria used for judgment, the Eagle-Appian-URSA venture had failed.

The basic elements of the CENCO-Eagle confrontation can be summarized in military-business terms. The symbols in Figure 5.2 are the same as those used in Figure 5.1.

CENCO could have accepted the status quo by holding (defending) in place, or it could have launched a limited expansion (attack) with an old product in the old marketplace. However, as did Napoleon at Ulm, CENCO chose to do otherwise. It did continue to offer a limited number of old products while, at the same time, it speeded up the development and introduction of the new computer. This one was intentionally designed to go beyond any of those planned by the Eagle combine. Like the allies at Ulm, the Eagle-Appian-URSA venture was out-gunned before it started.

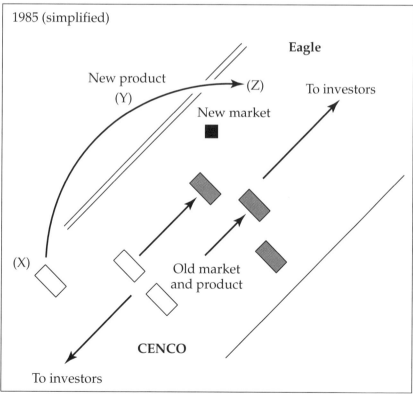

Figure 5.2 CENCO-Eagle Confrontation

One could raise the question of what better action the Austrian commander (or the Eagle chief executive) might have taken. As he had on a number of other things, Napoleon had ready opinions on such matters. He would have advised that the general, or the chief executive, say to himself many times in a day, "If the enemy should appear on the right or left, at the front or the rear, then what should I do?" If this is accepted as guidance, the answer for Eagle is clear. The first priority must be given to a detailed study of the competitor's capabilities and what can be done to meet an assault that could come from any direction. The old Chinese general Sun Tzu would have said much the same thing: The chief should first put his undertaking beyond the risk of failure. Having assured himself of this, he should then look for his opponent to make the first mistake. Sun Tzu did consider the possibility that an enemy would make no mistakes, but, in this situation, he felt neither commander would win. He did go on to explain that a general may know how to win but not be able to do so if the opportunity is never presented. For Sun Tzu, the conditions for winning are set by mistakes that are made by his opponents. On this, Napoleon would have disagreed. The Corsican was always quick to emphasize that the commander should protect himself from all likelihood of attack, but, having done this, he should create conditions that could generate their own opportunities. In fairness to these two masters, it may be argued that we are beating a cultural dead horse. Sun Tzu, the Asian, would counsel patience and a willingness to wait for the favorable moment. Bonaparte, the European, would expect to be more aggressive, and ready to change things when possible.

Actually, Sun Tzu's idea of waiting for an opponent's mistake is not unique to Eastern thinking. One modern author, in an article on how to win in the stock market, has referred to much of the action there as a "loser's game." In effect, he suggests that if you choose to play the market, you should take Sun Tzu's advice and first be sure to protect yourself; then you should study the rest of the action. The argument is, as before, that the only real way to win is through another's mistakes. In the stock market of today, this is based on the idea that the big money managers (institutional investors) already know the standard moves expected from their competitors. The smartest type of investors will always ensure they are well diversified and prepared for drops in the market. When the inevitable bad news comes, they will quickly cut their losses (before others react) and look for the next upturn in the market. Whoever makes the fewest mistakes will be most likely to come out ahead.

Napoleon, Sun Tzu, and many others speak of warfare as an art rather than a science. In one sense, the theater of operations is only a magnified canvas on which the campaign is painted. Certainly, the movement and positioning of Napoleon's army at Ulm is a classic painting by one of the greatest artists. The campaign is also an outstanding demonstration of the fact that strategy is concerned with events that take place away from the battlefield or the retail market. As it was at Ulm, the final outcome of a campaign may already have been determined when the basic moves have been made.

Strategy and Creative Thinking

For a moment, let us recap the logic at Ulm. A typical Napoleonic analysis might have begun by Napoleon's observing the terrain to the south of the Black Forest and the site of the Austrian positions. This area was bounded by lakes, streamlines, and mountains. To the north of the region in question is the Danube River. It soon becomes apparent, if the French chose to make a frontal attack, that the Austrians would be well prepared. If they decided to attack in the south, they would have to move in front of the Austrians and would be exposed to a flank attack that could force them up against the mountains. On the other hand, if they moved forward in the northern part of the zone (but south of the Danube River), they could be held against the river. The place that offered the best opportunity to move eastward was at the north of the river. Here they would have a much better chance to achieve surprise and safety from counterattack. This was also the critical place allowing them to threaten the supplies of the Austrian army and their line of communication extending back to Vienna. By concentrating a major force near Ulm, the French could then strike south and seize the critical area. That was the course of action they chose.

Clausewitz and Jomini describe the "decisive point" as the place or time where the success or failure of an entire operation is likely to be decided. During the campaign near Ulm, Napoleon did not spend his time wondering about what might happen to his other army in Italy. In the Austrian-Italian plan, it was anticipated that he would send more of his troops to Italy and weaken his strength in the north. Unfortunately for them, Napoleon did not think like Austrian or Italian generals. He saw that the key to the entire operation was in the geography of southern Germany, and there he focused his strength. As always, he kept the "big picture" in mind. Any of Mack's divisions could have defeated the French unit opposing them in the Black Forest, but the final outcome of the campaign would not be affected. The feint was made in the Black Forest region; the decisive point was at Ulm. It was there that the Austrian army was at most risk, and there that the victory was won.

In the end we come back to the concept of a few critical factors. A business may be successful with a hundred insignificant products and still lose a major market simply by neglecting some major products. Pareto's old rule is not yet out of date; it still serves to remind us that, in strategy, it is the pattern of a few important resources, actions, and objectives that determines the final outcome and eventually the reputation of an army or business enterprise.

The Austrian-Italian plan to defeat Napoleon in Germany seemed reasonable enough to ordinary thinkers, and it might have been quite successful against an ordinary general. Unfortunately, Napoleon did not fit into such a category. In fact, it would be hard to fit him into any of the common groups of strategists. He was, by all accounts, a military genius with creative thinking abilities that bypassed the average solution.

A somewhat structured approach to deciding strategy is presented in the army's *Estimate of the Situation*. Its format can also be used as a tool for business analysis. If chief executives followed its steps in detail, they would first make sure the mission is clearly stated. Next, they would study the environment in which they are operating, reviewing the facts and the whole situation. In the military estimate, all these factors are carefully analyzed and the actions that could be taken by the enemy are examined in greater detail. Simplified, these would include the likelihood of an enemy attack (as in a competitor aggressively seeking new customers), a defense (or hold in place), a withdrawal from action, and so on. After listing the possible enemy actions, the courses of action available to the friendly side are then subjected to study. These actions by our own units (e.g., a frontal attack, business expansion in an old market, etc.) are always closely scrutinized. Along with weighing each friendly action, the various enemy or competitor capabilities for meeting or frustrating them is also examined. After war-gaming the whole range of activities, the commander or chief executive would return to the list of actions he could take (e.g., envelop around the enemy flank, introduce a new product in the old market, introduce an old product in a new market, etc.), and then make his final decision.

One of the major necessities in this exercise is a search for new ideas or actions. These new ideas or actions are not likely to be a result of a superficial analysis. The greater probability is that they will emerge from an examination of ideas that initially show no connection; that is, they will only become apparent after a deliberate forcing of relationships not previously seen. Unfortunately, this requires a major effort and an avoidance of an age-old bias all of us have. We tend to be in the habit of trying to "make sense" of the world around us. Often, an entirely different type of thinking begins with a defiance of good sense. So, who can do this best? Who can generate new ideas? Actually, almost anyone can; the truly creative thinker is always hard to define. One effective strategist may be a detached dreamer who sees a host of new images in a tumble of passing clouds. Another may be only a learning machine with a memory of past actions that have worked on other occasions. In sum, a truly creative thinker may be simply a lucky soul who can look at the world from a new and different angle. "Shifting a paradigm in time may well save nine."

For most of us, the easiest road to creativity is probably in the assumption of the role of the critical listener alert for the new or the previously not known. Ideas that can turn our thinking into a new and different direction may come from many sources or emerge from a limited few. The problem is often one of making sure that the best sources can always be heard.

Sound opinions and fresh ideas can come from any level, from the lowest private soldier or factory worker, all the way to the top manager. Visits to the fighting area or to the working area can give an executive strategist access to a different person's thinking and perception of problems—a ready source of new insights. The summary statement here may be the following: Read everything you can, and visit everybody. Niccolo Machiavelli once wrote that a good general will listen to anyone who can tell him what he should do; he makes it a point to hear all of the different ideas and arguments before he makes a decision.

In a *Fortune* magazine article about interviewing the top manager of General Electric, the writer commented that the ideas being discussed might some day "rewrite the book on how to run a big company." For example, one of General Electric's policies was to find a market segment, or set of conditions, where the company could be number one, or at worst number two. With this approach to strategy, the chairman of General Electric would have had no difficulty in discussions with military field commanders in recent times or even in the distant past. Napoleon always thought in terms of finding the decisive point, a unique place and time that gave the greatest advantage. Once this was clearly determined, he focused the mass of his efforts there, determined to be number one.

During the American Civil War, General Nathan Bedford Forrest was asked about his rules for success on the battlefield, and he is said to have responded with something like, "It is really very simple, you get there the *fustest*, with the *mostest*." Napoleon, Clausewitz, Jomini, and the chief of General Electric would probably all give the same reply: Be stronger at the decisive point.

— 6 —

Be Certain They All Get the Word

The king of Wu once asked the great Chinese military sage, Sun Tzu, if his theories of warfare could be applied to women. When Sun Tzu replied that they could, the king ordered that several ladies of the court be assembled for a test. Sun Tzu divided them into two groups and placed one of the king's favorites at the head of each. Then he set about to explain the basic movements of military drill. Although the ladies appeared to understand the instructions, when the commands were given to begin the marching exercise, they seemed only amused by the orders and laughed aloud as he spoke. Sun Tzu paused and said, "If the words of command are not clear and distinct, if the orders are not thoroughly understood, then the general is to blame," and started the instruction over again. When the marching commands were given a second time, the result was more laughter. Then Sun Tzu said, "If the words of command are not clear and distinct, then the general is to blame. But if the orders are clear, and the soldiers nevertheless disobey, then it is the fault of their officers." With that, he ordered the two leaders beheaded.

To say the least, this is not what the king had in mind. He made haste to express confidence in Sun Tzu's ability to command troops and to give instruction, but that it was his desire that the punishment not be carried out. Sun Tzu replied that, having been given the responsibility of exercising command over the king's troops, he was duty bound to do so in the most efficient manner. He then ordered the sentence carried out. When the drill resumed, discipline was, understandably, much improved.

The example of Sun Tzu and the king has long been used by military writers to emphasize an important point. Though a general may be a country's leading expert on military operations and be in command, there may be some situations where those ranked above him might give orders that conflict with good military practice. The general must refuse to obey such orders, even those from the sovereign himself. Today, this principle is the subject of greater discussion, but one point of Sun Tzu's lesson is clear enough: the commander or chief executive must be certain in his own mind about what is to be done and then communicate this in the clearest possible terms.

An Image, but Inside a Head

A commander of a large military organization cannot personally fire every weapon or load all the trucks of an army in wartime. A chief executive officer cannot complete every sale or run every machine in the plant. In practice, all either one can do is talk. If a leader's instructions are not clearly stated or are not understood, and if the communication system does not work as it should, even when the decisions are very clear in the leader's own mind, an effort is doomed from the start.

Before a military or business manager can communicate intentions to lower-level managers, he or she must have a clear mental picture of the task to be performed and know what the staff can do. This can mean the processing of vast amounts of information on the situation at hand, on the background or past conditions, and on the possible future ahead. The problem of estimating future conditions is always a difficult one. There are competent managers who say that it cannot be done; they give little time to planning and tend to meet the world as it comes. There are others who claim that the future is mostly unpredictable; only the simplest plans can be made, and those only for short times ahead. Both groups will be wrong in some cases. Whether in formal planning sessions or by intermittent reviews, it is most likely that the chief executive is involved in some form of planning activity during most waking hours. He or she may be engaged in other activities at the moment, but the really important problems of the organization are never far from the chief executive's mind. One method such executives seem to employ can be compared to the computer routine once known as "time-sharing." The executive, like the computer, concentrates for a time on one situation (e.g., what went wrong in the last operation), then moves to another subject (e.g., a problem that may arise in the future). The chief performs only a partial study of one problem area before shifting to the next. As the time-sharing computer devotes only a fixed amount of time to one problem before it moves on to the next, so the executive might interrupt analysis to converse with a colleague or junior executive. Since this process continues throughout the working (and nonworking) day, there is an almost limitless number of breaks in activities in the commonplace world. The process thus tends to bounce back and forth between the active mode and the thinking or planning mode. This practice ties in with the view that the real value of planning lies not so much in the final product as in the mental exercise of analysis and speculation that helps one to work through a problem. It also seems that planning does not have to be expressed in words in order to exist, nor must planning be stated in detail to have any worth.

Any problem or its solution might be unclear at a certain time; the picture is always colored by the thinker's perceptions. Habit gives us both colors and cobwebs; it is not easy to brush them aside. During the Civil War, when General McClellan was commander of the Army of the Potomac, he seemed always to see General Lee's opposing army as much larger than it actually was and his own as always too weak, not ready to mount an attack. General Lee, from the opposite viewpoint, saw a hesitating General McClellan as an advantage for his Southern soldiers. It is not difficult to imagine the types of orders that would be issued by either commander. While General McClellan waited in place and asked President Lincoln for more troops, Lee often chose to move quickly in unexpected directions. This, of course, made McClellan even more uncertain and less likely to try to move forward. It is often the same in business.

After World War II, the chief executive of Montgomery Ward expected a major depression to hit the United States and felt it was wiser to wait before making new plans to expand. The managers at Sears, Roebuck and Co. saw a built-up demand for new products from the years of shortage and war. To meet an era of opportunities and growth, Sears made plans for its own expansion. In the years that followed, Ward would favor standing fast while they performed more study of business conditions. When Ward finally did decide to move, Sears had captured market share to the extent that Ward could not catch up.

As different perceptions of the battle situation will drive commanders in war, the differing perceptions of economic conditions give business strategists their personal views of the world. All this tends to make the chief executive's job especially difficult as he or she tries to become more objective in composing the clearest possible image of the situation before starting to describe it. The CEO must work especially hard to find good information both about the present and about the possibilities in the future before he or she can judge the situation or decide the actions to take. But this is only a start—even when the decision is made, it must be conveyed to others.

A Picture, Remade into Words

In spite of our awesome advances in science, we do not yet have the capability to transfer the exact contents of one brain to another. The first difficulty, of course, is getting an idea to the outside in a form that is clearly recognized by another human being. We are still very much dependent on a variety of methods for this translation, and the result is only a description—not quite an image itself. Again, however, this is only a step. Before an incoming thought can be understood, it needs to be reconstructed in the mind of the receiver from a pattern of many impressions.

New problems now face the recipient; the first is whether effective impressions have actually made an impact or only impacted the senses. A simple error in reading these signals has caused more than one chief executive to be misunderstood, sometimes even at great cost. Of course, the best of managers is always aware of these hazards, and efforts are made to avoid them. In the military, we hear tales (whether true or not) of the commander who kept an especially slow-witted officer on his staff to test whether orders were clear ("If Major So-and-so can understand it, for sure anyone can!"). Regardless of the origin of such stories, the point is still aptly made. If the message can be misunderstood, it is possible that it will be.

A variety of visual and verbal techniques are used to overcome the difficulties of effective communication. Military trainers are renowned for their use of visual aids, and the use of maps is especially important. Frederick the Great's first priority in any campaign was to find a good map of the region. Photographs, sketches, and other visual aids can often be used to help to convey the basic idea without an excess of details. Many such aids are quite useful in explaining concepts, but complex thinking and discussion require elaboration and sometimes even more verbiage. Although a picture may well be worth a thousand words, there is sometimes more to the story than a thousand words can muster.

While words and pictures can improve the clarity of ideas being transmitted, numbers can also aid understanding. In spite of the long-held movie tradition, most armies do not order their troops to "attack at dawn"; they favor a time on the clock. The word *dawn* could mean sunrise, first light, early light, good visibility, or a dozen other things not intended. Problems can also be caused by misstating or leaving out an important number or word in a message. In combat, soldiers sometimes attempt to reduce transmission errors by repeating the critical sections (e.g., "0400 Hours— I say again—0400 Hours . . ."). A mistake in a rifle company's request for ten men or twenty boxes of ammunition might not be crucial to a field army's operation, but the incorrect arrival date of twenty shiploads of supplies is an entirely different matter.

The use of familiar or standard terms helps to ensure that a message will be understood. There are many terms that are easily interpreted by both military and business practitioners, but differences also exist. For example, the phrase "chain of command" is used by both types of practitioners to describe the channel of communication running from the top to the lower levels of an organization, but the expression "base of operations" can have different implications depending on whether it is used in the military or in business.

One advantage of the use of standardized terms is that they can be learned by new members when they first come to the organization and are soon understood by everyone. During the American Revolution, one of the most important contributions made to the struggling new Continental Army was that of General von Steuben, who insisted on developing and implementing standard systems of drill. Before a set of common terms and movements was published, regiments from New York and Virginia were organized and trained to maneuver in a manner quite different from those of Connecticut or Maryland; units from North Carolina had problems following instructions for plans and operations that were clearly understood in Pennsylvania and New Jersey. After Valley Forge, the officers and men of the Continental Army had a common fighting language, and, for the first time, the common regulation of fire and direction for combat maneuvers was clearly understood by all of Washington's army.

Many problems of communication and coordination can exist between subordinate units, even when the best efforts to avoid those problems are made. In World War II, a story is told that telephone traffic between the U.S. and British troops in North Africa was disrupted because of a language (yes, language) problem. It was obvious that the switchboard operators on both sides spoke some form of the English language, but when they used the expression "Are you through?" each one got a different message. Some Americans used the phrase to find out if the line was free (i.e., the person was off the line or had finished the conversation). If the Britisher answered "yes," the Yank would pull the plug. This was very disconcerting to the U.K. soldier responding, because he thought the question was "Do you have a good connection, are you plugged through to the other party?" Allied radio-telephone procedures were later changed to "Have you finished?" an expression they all seemed to know.

Try Looking in Section Three

In the layout of a daily newspaper, the editorial page usually stays in the same part of the paper. By standardizing policies and procedures, any organization can do much to improve efficiency and reduce the time wasted or lost. In organizational communication, standardization can certainly save writing space, simplify messages, aid in the prompt execution of orders, and speed up reporting procedures. An example is the military unit that uses a standard loading and movement plan for its trucks; it might be put into action by a simple message or code (e.g., "Execute HOW ABLE"). A manufacturing firm might have a checklist on actions involved in plant closings to ensure that everyone in the company is kept informed and that community input is given consideration.

The use of a standardized pattern for presenting routine information can establish a common mind-set for all the likely receivers of a message. With a uniform format, each section of a military order is tied to a specific topic and provides a quick and simple checklist for clarity and completeness. If a unit commander knows that information on the enemy situation is always stated in the first paragraph of his instructions, it is easy for him to see when appropriate information is missing. In business, this approach has been used in feasibility studies, staff reports, and other communications that require a problem discussion and recommendations. Aside from the obvious advantage of ensuring that key factors are not overlooked, it also speeds up reading time and improves reading efficiency.

Military orders issued in the field have long been in a standard format that can serve as a checklist of important items. The form for a combat order is quite simple and can be adapted to a variety of different operations. In business, as in the military, such a format can help to keep instructions clear while allowing action flexibility by those who are well trained in their jobs. An example of how such a form might be used is shown in Figure 6.1.

This form is an example of a general plan of action and outlines major factors in formulating and executing a strategy. The first part gives a brief review of the situation and is followed by a mission statement. That mission statement describes the strategy or how the mission will be accomplished. The execution paragraph begins with a statement of the general concept of the operation and then supplies the details to the subordinate units. The concept of the operation shows a parallel between military and business thinking; both move from a general concept to descriptions in greater detail. This is an approach reminiscent of Napoleon's habit of starting with a broad view of the situation to begin a strategic analysis. Successful business chief executives seem to use this same wide sweep-then-focus approach when they consider a range of opportunities, and then narrow the study down to concentrate on a market or sector. The concept of the operations is, in both cases, only the broadest outline; details are filled in later. These additions include information on the objectives to be assigned, the resources available, and a summary of action expected. The form is clearly an organizing framework for analyzing a problem and the statement of a plan for its solution.

Standard formats such as this can be used to emphasize critical factors and reduce excess verbiage. Users of such formats seek to capitalize on prior knowledge and help to increase the visual impact of maps, charts, and diagrams. In an ideal situation, the body

COMPANY HEADING
Location

___

Date/Time/Year

1. ENVIRONMENT
   a. General Economy and Forecast
   b. Industry Conditions
   c. Competitive Situation

2. MISSION
   a. Provide—— (Product/Service)
   b. To—— (Market)

3. EXECUTION
   a. Concept of Business Operation (Strategy)
   b. Northern Division
      i. Objectives (Sales)
      ii. Resources (Budget)
      iii. Actions (Methods and Mix)
   c. Southern Division
      i. Objectives (Sales)
      ii. Resources (Budget)
      iii. Actions (Methods and Mix)
   d. Priorities
      i. New Products/Services
      ii. Costs (with Sales and Budget)
      iii. Miscellaneous (Practices, Ethics, etc.)

4. ADMINISTRATION
   a. Finance
   b. Purchasing
   c. Maintenance
   d. Personnel
   e. Miscellaneous

5. COMMUNICATION
   a. Reports, E-mail, Fax, etc.

___

Signed: Abe Cdefg, CEO

Figure 6.1   Communication Format

of the form would be used only for the essential items of information and guidance; most specific details would be left to front-line executives.

Hearing Doesn't Mean Doing

An assumption is often made that the receiver of a message is already motivated and ready to execute the instructions received—all the receiver lacks is knowledge of what has to be done. If the actions are simple and instructions have only to be memorized, there may not be any problem. The soldiers of Frederick of Prussia's time had long practice in the execution of the movements and were skilled in the manual of arms. They could maneuver more quickly than their opponents and generate much greater firepower. Any deviation from standard practice resulted in drastic punishment. One problem with such a tightly controlled system is that, when anything unusual occurs, no one knows what to do (and no one takes the initiative to do something). During the time of the Seven Years' War, it was enough to know the movements that might be ordered; today we would expect to know why. If the action individual has an understanding of the general situation, he can see where a change might be effective and help others with a part of the task. Knowing the broader picture, even the lowest worker can do his job better and more easily fit in with the group. On the other hand, if the workers and their supervisors are not convinced that the plan will succeed, the project will certainly fail.

This broader scope of job orientation is essential for the modern self-managed team. It includes knowledge of the unit's background and mission (to provide a certain product or service), the types of problems they can face (especially those with competitors), and common examples of solutions (e.g., different work methods and products). On the battlefield, a combat leader has limited time to review the action, but his troops still need to know what must happen and how the team will meet the objective.

The chief is always concerned about whether the message is getting through either to the workers or to the troops at the front. If the person on the end of the communication chain has a clear idea of what is intended by the instructions, it seems reasonable that those in the middle are just as correctly informed. Unfortunately, it is not completely unusual for a message to be revised or knowingly delayed at various points in the chain. It is better to find out early when this is the case, since changing established policies in a large organization can be both difficult and time consuming. When exposed to new ideas, some members of an organization are always slow to respond to them—and even slower to accept them. The chief executive of one company said he was eight years into the process of selling corporate change and still trying to make greater progress. It is not surprising that one of the lessons taught by Sun Tzu and the ladies of the court is that if the message is not clear at the lowest level, the project will always take up more time. The women selected for training did not seem to see the importance of discipline and close cooperation or to grasp what their role was to be. Lacking this level of understanding, they would be very unlikely to accept the notion that they should be reeducated and expected to fight in a war. If these problems exist with good instructions, the likelihood of success with poor instructions or practice will be much closer to zero.

One way to see if the message got through is to visit the lowest unit and observe it as it goes into action. This is an excellent reason for the commander to inspect his troops at the front, but there are also quite a few others. He may wish to pass on recent information or obtain the quickest feedback. He may want to show his interest in what the troops are doing and help in cheering them on. He may need to obtain more information on the subordinate leaders' activities or show them he is backing their efforts. Napoleon undoubtedly considered all of these. His usual practice was to give orders that would focus his units on a decisive point, and then he would go forward to be there himself. This allowed him to make certain that 1) his orders had been understood, 2) he had the latest information on the situation, and 3) he was in the best position to decide on future actions.

Orders, Details, and Staffs

In a fluid or obscure combat situation, a "mission type" of order is often appropriate. Here, a major unit (e.g., an armored division) might be directed simply to follow an axis of advance (e.g., west, guiding along National Highway 462) rather than staying within the right and left boundaries that can be marked on a map. In this manner, the local commander is given more freedom to evaluate and react to a new situation. Alternatively, a unit may be ordered to delay an enemy force for a specified period of time or to hold forward of a line on the ground. In both cases, the emphasis is on flexibility of action and is somewhat comparable to the business technique called management by objectives. Here the stress is on the objectives to be reached, leaving to the manager's judgment just what is to be done, and how.

The mission type of order may be used at the corporate level to provide general guidance when, because of a changing situation, details are not likely to be appropriate. If the senior executive is experienced in his field and familiar with standard procedures, the basic strategy can be stated in very few words. In many situations, a one-page plan of strategy can serve better than a thick, imposing volume locked up in the company safe. In World War II, the directive ordering General Eisenhower to invade the continent of Europe was contained in a single paragraph.

There is always a question about how much detail is necessary, and few chief executives can state their intentions in such clear language that no misunderstanding is possible. Napoleon routinely issued early action orders in which his corps commanders were told to move to a specific place on the ground, then prepare to attack on his order. Some critics contend that the instructions were too restrictive, that he did not allow for personal initiative and stifled original thinking. Jomini mentions one of Napoleon's generals who, not having orders to do more than move to a forward location, passed up an opportunity to attack a disorganized enemy force nearby. Even Louis Berthier, the chief of staff for many years, was criticized when he refused to vary from a letter of instruction given him by Napoleon, even when it caused obvious problems in execution and seemed to contradict its own purpose. In defense of Bonaparte's actions, it could be said that security requirements often forced him to limit the amount of information he was willing to hazard in print (and then again, who can argue with success?). His emphasis on concentration and mass made it essential to emphasize secrecy in movement and control procedures.

The publication of a military order usually takes place at the headquarters of the senior commander. The order is often given by oral announcement then copied in written form. This serves both to clarify a number of details and to provide a permanent record. Most of the details are covered in later orders prepared and distributed by the staff. Because the general staff works directly with the maker of strategy, Jomini felt that the chief of staff should be an officer with broad experience who is familiar with all branches of war. As might be expected, Napoleon often acted as his own chief of staff, but, in the normal pattern of duties, it was Berthier, his senior staff member, who prepared and issued the orders.

Aside from the normal contingent of staff officers, military organizations also include a number of liaison officers who deliver the high-priority messages and act as special agents for the obtaining of information at special locations and units. In business, these liaison specialists would probably be described as project researchers or area specialists.

While the staff is an important means of communication, there are also some interpretive hazards that can show up in its functions. For example, a casual visitor might observe a general staff officer giving instructions to a subordinate commander and assume that the orders are from the staff officer himself. This is never the case; the messenger must not be confused with the chief. Those in the military system know that the staff officer has authority only to present the orders for the general or commander; if asked, the officer may try to explain the instructions, but only as he understands the senior commander's intent.

The staff officer always works for the chief executive, but this does not mean that he cannot be of considerable value to any subordinate unit. The effectiveness of an ideal staff officer comes about through a wide range of experience, access to critical information, and a unique knowledge of the views and personality of the senior commander he represents. In general, a good staff officer sees his work as supporting the entire organization.

The effectiveness of an organization is dependent not only on vertical channels of communication but also on lateral or between-unit links that can simplify the task of coordination. A lack of information exchange between subordinate units and their headquarters can be very costly, even embarrassing at times. An example of this occurred in 1862 in the Shenandoah Valley, where Stonewall Jackson conducted one of the most brilliant campaigns of the Civil War. The trace of this valley runs generally southwest to northeast along the western boundary of modern Virginia, and at the northern end it meets the Potomac River at a place that is within striking distance of the nation's capital. It was partly because of this access to the river and the seat of government that President Lincoln took special pains to see that Washington was well protected.

For the South, Jackson's mission in 1862 was to keep the maximum number of Union forces occupied and away from northern Virginia. His campaign, designed to do this, is still a classic example of the use of limited resources to accomplish a strategic objective. He used the utmost secrecy to deprive the Union generals of information, and he used a series of rapid movements to strike at places and times not expected. As a consequence of his activities, the Northern generals were, time and again, confused about the whereabouts of his army. To make matters worse, they were often less than effective in keeping each other informed.

An action that took place at Strasburg, Virginia, provides a vivid example. There were two Union army units: one consisting of 35,000 men was on the west side of the town, and another of 15,000 men was on the east side. They were in an ideal position to trap Jackson and his troops between them. What actually happened gives a shining example of why Stonewall Jackson was so highly regarded as a general. By aggressive use of his cavalry in the west and a deliberate feint in the east, he was able to keep the two Union commanders so confused and inept in coupling their efforts that his entire seven-mile-long supply train passed safely between the two enemy divisions. Jackson and his soldiers thus escaped unharmed and rode back to rejoin Lee's army. While the business world may not have such graphic examples as this, the problems are still much the same. In almost any company, a lack of information exchange between two or more subunits (e.g., marketing and production) can result in a loss of sales or serious and costly delays. The situation becomes especially critical when the company is faced with aggressive competitors having greater human and financial resources or when subordinates are improperly trained and unwilling to help other units.

On the day that the women of Wu were selected for drill, the king and Sun Tzu were both speaking proper Chinese but looking in different directions. On a winter day in 1957, William Hewlett and David Packard did not have the Chinese problem. They had assembled a few top managers of the Hewlett-Packard company to focus on where they might go in the future. Company sales at that time were around $30 million, and income was near $2 million. In their discussions at this important meeting, they reorganized the company and set out some rules that would guide it.

One of the concepts they settled on was management by objectives. This notion stresses a mutual give and take of information between the senior manager and each of his chosen subordinates. The intention is to develop a common understanding of the resources available, the objectives to be reached, and the freedom of action allowed.

Another of their principles became known as management by walking around. It was based on the idea that higher-level managers would spend more time on the factory floor discussing with the workers where the company was heading and what could be done to improve the company. This is the same as the idea of the commander's visit with his troops at the front. Managers and commanders are each seeking to reach an objective.

By the 1980s, Hewlett-Packard was many times larger than it had been in 1957. It had sales of over $8 billion and profits of $600 million. After thirty years of the project they were still walking and talking and growing and looking for ways to improve.

— 7 —

Go to the Sound of the Guns

Sometime after two o'clock in the afternoon of 27 July 1675, near Salzbach, Germany, a single cannon shot ended the life of a Frenchman named Turenne. He was 64 years of age, an officer of long service and dedication to his country.

Turenne is certainly not an overworked name in the writings of American historians. In this country it would be difficult to find as many as three books about him in English; hence, few of our military historians have devoted space to his battles. In France it is quite a different story. His full name was Prince Henri de la Tour d'Auvergne, Vicomte de Turenne, Maréchal-Général of the King's Camps and Armies and Colonel-General of the Light Cavalry. A simple description of his position was that he ranked above all other generals in the army of Louis XIV. His capability as a strategist was far ahead of his time. As a leader for the common soldier, few were considered his peers. One day he could be a personal advisor to the king; on another, a leader of soldiers in battle. A teacher of warfare to nobility, he was also much loved by the common people.

A Model for Men, a Teacher for Kings

Turenne's uniqueness lay in part in his unselfish dedication to his country and to the soldiers who served with him. He was admired as a commander in battle and respected for his character in peace and in war. Many observers have described him as a firm but considerate army commander, modest perhaps to a fault, always generous to others, asking nothing for himself. Napoleon spent much time studying Turenne and looked on him as a model for leadership. A quick comparison of these two can provide an interesting study.

From his early days in the Italian War, Napoleon seemed to know he was destined to rule. Turenne, even in his last battle for France, was guided only by a strong sense of responsibility and dedication to the service of others. Napoleon left no doubt that he was to be treated as a very important person; unquestioned obedience was expected. Turenne also left no doubt that he would demand instant obedience in battle, but, in any other environment, he could be best described as a humble individual. He did exercise the prerogatives of his rank at court, but this may have been more to ensure that the position of his family and its name would be respected than that any rights accrue to him as a person. Napoleon rewarded his generals with titles and gifts of property; Turenne did not have the titles to give even if he had desired to do so. His family was of high rank but not of great wealth, and, by the standards of his peers, he lived within modest means. Over the period of his military career he actually gave away much of his personal wealth to the officers and troops who served with him. On at least one occasion he had his personal silverware cut into pieces and used to pay his troops because the government did not come through with their pay. When he was honored by appointment to the country's highest military rank, Marshal of France, he asked for no new titles or lands. He asked only for those lands that had been taken from his family many years before during a political conflict with the king.

In the conduct of military affairs, Bonaparte and Turenne had access to quite different levels of human and material resources. From 1804 on, Napoleon was the ruler of France and could call on whatever resources the country had available. Alexander, Gustavus Adolphus, and Frederick II were also heads of state and rulers of their respective state's wealth. Caesar in Gaul and Hannibal in Italy were under little or no restriction from their home governments and could utilize whatever materials they might find in the theater of operations. Turenne was always under whatever restrictions might be imposed upon him by the king and hence forced to compete with others for the necessary arms and men. While many of the other great commanders held positions comparable (in business) to a chairman of the board of directors, Turenne was more akin to a company president under a very active chairman (the king) with many ideas of his own.

Napoleon and Turenne both displayed an uncommon knowledge of the value of focusing their strength against the enemy's weakness, of skillful positioning of units, and of rapid maneuver (usually by way of envelopment) with frequent use of surprise. They appeared to agree less on the nature of the end game. Napoleon sought to destroy the enemy or at least render him ineffective. Turenne was not likely to carry an action beyond what was necessary to claim a recognized victory. However, it must be noted that many different cultural norms were also playing a part. During Turenne's lifetime, the common practice was to maneuver for position and force the enemy to withdraw. Cutting or threatening supply lines or lines of communication, forcing the enemy to retreat, was usually sufficient for a declaration of victory. Both sides made an effort to avoid a prolonged period of contact that could cause major losses to either side. This was a time of the use of many foreign mercenaries, and the hiring of seasoned veterans or even the finding and training of new soldiers could make it all quite expensive. The fewer veterans lost in an engagement, so much the better for each side. There were also other problems regarding how wars were fought; some were built into the system by pressures from the ministers of the king and others who served in his court. In spite of these problems, however, a critical influence on the action was a commander's concern for his soldiers.

Turenne, like many other great men, seemed to continue learning through all of the years of his life. He improved with each new battle, and his last campaign in Alsace is considered one of his best.

In many ways, it can serve as a simple review of the best type of thinking in strategy.

A Masters Class for Generals

By the late 1600s, King Louis XIV was claiming much of the land that is now included within the boundaries of France. In the northeast it faced the Spanish Netherlands (now Belgium). On the eastern front were the provinces of Lorraine (near Luxemburg), Alsace, and Franche-Comté. In 1674, the French claims to these areas were being disputed by an alliance of countries along the eastern border. As the year drew to a close, the Elector of Brandenburg, with armies from the German states, had crossed the Rhine River at Strasbourg and occupied northern Alsace. Against the Elector's army of 50,000 men, Turenne, with only 20,000 troops, was forced to delay and then fall back to wait for reinforcements. By November he was able to build up to 33,000 men but decided to fall back again to the region of Haguenau and Savergne. The allies, confident of their ability to hold the territory west of the Rhine, chose to consolidate their positions and go into winter quarters. The wily old fox of France was not ready to quit for the season (see Figure 7.1).

Instead of continuing to face the larger force head on, Turenne decided to march south and away from the face of his enemy. He would be keeping the mountains to his left and looking for a gap through which he could enter Alsace. At Belfort he found that place. After defeating the Elector outposts there and at Mulhouse, he turned north toward the larger contingent at Colmar. A brief reconnaissance there convinced him of the value of a dominant hill mass at Turkheim, just west of the Colmar defenses. The Germans had ignored this section of terrain in their defensive preparations; they considered it to be inaccessible. It was already too late when they discovered that Turenne had placed his troops in position there and was preparing to use the high ground to increase the French advantage. From the front, his infantry struck the German main positions with two columns; from the heights at Turkheim he rolled back their weakened right flank. The final result was that the Germans were

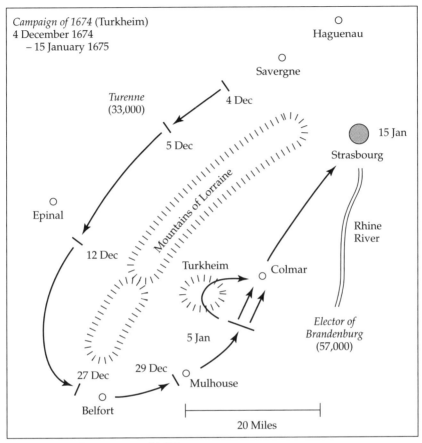

Figure 7.1   Campaign of 1674

forced back to defenses at Strasbourg, and the Elector saw fit to with-draw to the other side of the Rhine. In approximately one month, with a force little more than half the enemy strength, Turenne had beaten the Elector's army and regained Alsace for France.

In the engagements of 1674, as he had in countless others, Turenne demonstrated an unusual ability to create, plan, and execute campaigns at two different levels of action, and do so with minimum losses. In this campaign, one can easily trace on the map the strategic envelopment that he used to concentrate greater strength on a weaker part of the Elector's scattered army. He then plotted the succession of lesser battles as well as the tactical flanking movement that struck from the hills at Turkheim. It was clear that Turenne saw the entire region with the eyes of a master planner and then carried out the separate details in the role of a combat leader. He marched to the south as a strategist and fought back to the north as tactician.

What Turenne did at Turkheim was what he had always done and only requires a few words to describe. He studied the situation from his own viewpoint as well as from the viewpoint of the enemy, chose a strategy that would give him the greatest advantage, coordinated the separate elements, and went forward to support the action.

Turenne was killed a few months after the victory at Turkheim. The occasion of his death provides some interesting insights into the different perceptions of various individuals and groups viewing a single man.

In the confusion that immediately followed Turenne's death, the other generals worked to regroup the army, but the rank and file of soldiers were most impatient to avenge their beloved commander. Turenne's horse was a mare named Magpie, and it is said that some of his troops began shouting, "Let Magpie go forward, she will lead us." (Riderless but ever forward to the battle.)

In his will, Turenne had directed that he be buried with as little ceremony as possible in the commune where he had died, but Louis XIV simply refused to allow it. He ordered that a special service be held in the cathedral of Notre Dame and directed that the burial be at Saint-Denis, which, at that time, was reserved for the Bourbon kings. Over 100 years later, when Napoleon was the First Consul of France, he ordered that Turenne's casket be moved to the site of Les Invalides. There it remains today, just a few steps away from the sarcophagus of the great Napoleon himself.

Leadership and the Strategist

Napoleon contended that a good general should have a thorough knowledge of his field, sound judgment, physical courage, a strong sense of responsibility, and fairness toward his fellow man. In his view, mental and moral characteristics were desirable in equal measure. He looked upon Turenne as being as close to this ideal as a general could hope to be, because, as a senior military officer, he was highly regarded as an expert and teacher in many important fields. He was also an outstanding leader, well known to common soldiers as the "father of his troops." The title is especially interesting when we recall that a large percentage of troops in those days were hired as mercenaries from countries other than France, and their allegiance was primarily to whoever provided their pay. These were not the same kinds of soldiers that Napoleon would conscript and lead after the Revolution—those were willing to fight "for the glory of France." In Turenne's case it seemed to make little difference. He had established a reputation such that his troops, of whatever background, knew he would lead them to victory and would not expose them to more danger than he found to be absolutely necessary.

We have discussed the role of the strategist in his role as a general in the previous pages. The need for a leader in strategic action is not always easy to see. The strategist thinks in terms of the mission and of all the means he or she will have to accomplish it; the leader's focus is on the many sub-tasks that mark the way toward the objectives and on the people who see to it that they are accomplished. Yet, in another sense, a good strategist must also be a good leader; only the emphasis has changed. The strategist considers many types of resources; the leader starts with the people alone. The strategist looks for a series of integrated actions to match the multiple objectives and means. A leader focuses on one objective at a time and guides individuals and groups to reach it.

It seems clear that an understanding of leadership is essential to the top manager for a number of very important reasons. Managers' duties often make them responsible for the selection and training of leaders and the assignment or future change of those in leadership positions. But what is even more important is that they must set the example and be a model for those who would become their leaders.

Just what is this thing we call leadership? Today there are dozens of views, some more complex than others. As a much simplified case of the concept, we could imagine an open hillside and a group of weekend hikers who are on their way to a camp. The members of the club have never climbed the hill before, nor have they seen the new camping area. Their guide, some distance ahead of the group, has already reached the hilltop and can see the hikers behind him on one side and the campsite on the other. The hikers are not worried about which direction they take; they are sure that their guide knows the area and will lead them on to the camp.

Or, in a little different environment, one can think of the stage of a theater prepared for an evening concert (the task) to be performed by a symphony orchestra (the group). The conductor (the leader), like the hikers' guide, will be a focus of the members of a musical team as they take their seats or positions. In this particular case there are many highly trained individuals, each with a special skill, but the problem of guidance and coordination still remains to be solved. Although the musicians have long been familiar with their parts in the plan (the work), they are still aware of the need for guidance. Each one has his own particular task, but they all look to a competent leader to put the pieces together for the maximum effect of the whole.

In both of these examples we can see three basic elements in leadership, and all of them must be understood fully. Each one depends on the others; the concept becomes a three-legged stool. In order that leadership be effective, the task must be clearly identified, the group must have the required skills, and, perhaps most important, there must be a point of focus—the leader—to guide the task to completion. Good leadership here is an effective integration of a task, a group, and a leader.

The Task.   A special job of the strategist is to translate the mission of the organization into sub-tasks for a number of different groups. These tasks must be designed for the unique capability of each sub-unit and still fit in with the basic structure and mission. For example, the general task of the military is to defend the country. The mid-range task is to win campaigns. The short-range task is to reach each of the local objectives. In business, the general task is to meet the needs of contributors, especially those of the customers. The mid-range task is to achieve success in a particular part of the market. The short-range tasks are basically the same as they are in the military; they involve leading the groups of key workers in a multitude of activities (e.g., selling, production, etc.) that lead to market success. Whatever the task, the members of each of the groups must understand the overall purpose and their own role in achieving it.

We have already pointed out that the strategist must take into account a great range of actions that will make for strategic success. In business, these start with an orientation toward the customer and a provision of a product or service. Groups involved in these efforts include the headquarters personnel, the general and special supporting agencies, the middle managers, and countless troops at the front. Many others who can be critical to the effort may not appear on the payroll: a broker who sells the company's stocks and bonds, the banker who handles the loan, an official of a government bureau that helps to regulate the industry, and so on.

The Group.   An army commander or corporate chief executive is responsible for a long list of groups, often all at one time. A parallel responsibility of any leader includes all the members of these groups—for example, the employees and the investors of a firm considered separately and together.

Each group and the members of it have their own unique points of view, and the leaders' and workers' responsibilities in their jobs (and in the group) must be seen against a background that includes the culture involved. Today, for example, it is common for a military officer or business executive to operate in a number of different countries. In the United States, the individual is considered very important; the worker expects to be looked on as a person with particular talents and needs. In Japan, the group (e.g., the family, ancestors, the company, etc.) often has a higher status; individuals are more likely to be viewed and also forced by custom to view themselves as expendable for the good of the team or group.

Differences in these perceptions are quite evident when viewed across international borders, but the question of how groups and their members may perceive themselves and their workplaces are clearly visible inside every country. An engineer and an anthropologist, both looking at the remains of an ancient village, can see different forms of evidence and hence come to different conclusions about those remains. A Methodist and a Moslem presented with the same human problem (e.g., crime, health, etc.) might not always find the same solution. The outlook of the college-trained financial analyst may differ from that of a self-taught investor. What is most important for the present discussion is that sensitive top-level managers will soon understand that their perceptions of the worker's job is not the same as the worker's perception. The best manager is always aware of the difference and tries to compensate for it.

Whatever the cultural differences may be, there are still some basic notions that apply to all group members as human beings. Most people in any culture will try to conform their behavior to norms accepted by those in the group. In fact, banishment or rejection from the group is considered a severe punishment. It is still in use today, especially for those incarcerated in prison. Solitary confinement is the ultimate in social isolation.

The Leader.   There are those who feel that leadership can best be described with a list of personal characteristics or traits. Presumably these traits will distinguish the outstanding leader from the opposite, the non-leader (a follower cannot be taken as the opposite of a leader, because the leader and the follower are both oriented in the same direction). A number of investigations have shown that when you ask different individuals to make a list of good leadership characteristics, there is likely to be little agreement when all of the lists are compared. There are three hypotheses that may account for this: 1) There are no common traits, 2) leadership is too complex to be described with a simple listing of traits, or 3) the pattern of traits that are needed may change with the situation. Up to the present time, we have not been able to prove or disprove the first two possibilities and so are often left with the third—each situation is different and a new set of abilities may be required for a leader to succeed at each new task. On the other hand, there is some conflict with the commonsense view that certain characteristics are an enduring part of one's personality. Confucius once asked, "How can a man change his character, how can a leopard change his spots?" It does seem unlikely that the leader would need to change his or her personality each time he or she tries a new task. A part of the problem may be related to definitions and how we commonly use them. Descriptions of personality, in particular, can lead us in two different directions. In one, the individual is described in terms of what he or she is (composition) and amounts to a listing of traits. Another definition can be stated in terms of what the individual does (common behavior patterns). With these two modes of descriptions, one could also describe an automobile—a composition of metal, rubber, plastics, and glass (what it is) or as a transporter of people and things (what it does). To apply the analogy to leadership, we could speak of the leader in terms of characteristics (e.g., strong, confident, decisive, aggressive, etc.) or in terms of behaviors (e.g., looks for facts, defines problems, states challenges, etc.). Both viewpoints seem to have validity and will probably be widely used until better methods are found.

There is always the possibility that a few less appealing traits might be balanced with more appealing ones in the same personality and hence the composite will be hard to describe. A leader may not present a clear set of characteristics that will endear him or her at first glance but, in time, will show a consistent pattern of actions that come to hold our respect. We have all worked for an individual whom we disliked as a person, but we found we could still give credit for what he or she did on the job. Not many of us can claim to be perfect, and the overall impression—the pluses and minuses together—is what we see in a person. As Machiavelli pointed out to the Prince, "If you can't have them both, it is better to be respected (e.g., for knowing how to get the job done) than to be loved (e.g., for always being a good guy in the group)."

Even with all the problems involved in the use of words to describe a leader, there does seem to filter through a suggestion of a list of traits that describe a leader. Several research reports have shown that common terms such as *honesty, knowledge,* and *responsibility* somehow end up on the list. What this may really mean is that the leader (as guide) must first be seen as a standard for behavior, a respected and consistent reference that can be used by the group. The group members want to be assured, for example, that the leader will "tell it like it is," that they "know where she stands," or that he will not "waffle or hedge." They may not like everything he or she says, but they want to have confidence in what the leader will do. Ideally, they would come to believe that the leader will get the job done and still have their best interest at heart. We may summarize these comments by concluding that the leader must be consistent, knowledgeable about the task at hand, and considerate of those in the group.

Charles Ardant du Picq, a French military officer and writer, argued that confidence in their comrades and in their chief is what makes a group of soldiers into a fighting team. He saw that when this confidence was lacking, some of the most impressive warriors of their times (e.g., both the Chinese and the Mongols, known for not fearing death) did not hold up when fighting against well-led and disciplined troops. Without effective leadership even the bravest individuals can become disorganized, disoriented, and totally ineffective.

Just how much a leader's presence is worth can be difficult to guess. The Duke of Wellington is to have said he estimated that Napoleon's presence on the battlefield could be like adding 40,000 more troops.

Encouraging the Troops at the Front

Some managers seem to feel that the ideal top executive must step up and lead every action in person—show that he or she can run a turret lathe or knows how to service a truck. A demonstration of such ability would, no doubt, gain the workers' attention and probably increase their respect, but executives doing this type of leading may be using up time they cannot afford to lose. They can often accomplish just as much by asking an appropriate question to show interest in the job being done, and then let the worker or soldier show how well he or she can do the job. The critical action on the part of the senior manager is to show an interest in the concerns of the troops at the front. A real interest in the activities of the workplace is hard to pretend, especially when tried at long distance.

The chief executive of an organization usually makes visits to the field to get more information on the situation and to show interest in those at the front rather than to reveal how much he or she personally knows about each task. These visits may appear to take too much time, but nothing can replace them in either the process of judging the situation or in the process of affecting the morale and attitude of the front-line workers or troops. Even in rear areas or in peacetime, a command visit, which is the cause for intense preparation by troops and stressful to sub-unit leaders, can bring a welcome sense of relief providing that lift in morale for a job well done. The troops may not want to know every detail of the grand strategy that brought them to the battlefield, but they will always remember the big commander who came forward to see how they were doing and recognized their achievement.

As with human activities, the effects of inspections can be intensified by surprise; an unscheduled visit from the "big boss" gets everyone's attention. Some chief executives schedule them for the stated purpose of a formal "inspection," while the real purpose is to recognize an outstanding effort. It is ironic that these "cheerleading" visits may be most needed just when time is hardest to find.

As always, the matter of priorities must be scrutinized carefully. A senior executive is limited in the types and number of personal visits she can make in a given day. She cannot spend all her time at the headquarters, at the workplace, or at the front. She would be wrong to attempt to manage a sizable enterprise from the side of an assembly line. A picture of the senior commander stepping forward to lead the troops in an infantry attack may make for good movie footage, but he is probably also placing the entire operation at risk. The reason is simple—when leading the charge, he becomes, at best, a good rifleman. Leading a combat unit is job enough for one man; he cannot keep track of an entire army. If he is leading its charge, it is impossible for him to keep informed about all the other activities for which he is still responsible. The senior commander should often appear at the front, not to show he can lead the attack, but to encourage other leaders who, it is hoped, will then take action to do so.

Personal example and bravery are not at question here. It is a question of how the best job can be done. In a football game, the coach does not get out on the playing field; he does not have to prove he can play. The important thing to remember about the presence and attention of a senior executive is that it places more emphasis on the effort at a particular time and place. After a few visits from a top manager, even the dullest subordinate will get the message, "troops do well what the commander inspects."

Perhaps because of its obvious impact, the emphasis on top management is sometimes overdone. This assertion is made in spite of scholars who say that the best way to solve a particular problem is to have the senior manager give it a top priority. We have already agreed that this is usually true, but the application can be overdone. When too many things are emphasized, the result is that nothing is emphasized. The real priorities cease to exist, and a new ranking process must be started again.

There is always a need for the cheerleader visit. While it is easy to dismiss these as useless exercises and not necessary in a unit run by professionals, the subject is much more complex. Practically everyone recognizes the value of special occasions, such as holding recognition ceremonies and giving awards, but there is also a separate place for the regular and honest show of interest in the efforts of the troops. These must be a part of the normal activities in the executive day, deliberate, but without undue ceremony. When the chief executive works at demonstrating a genuine concern for the sub-unit's problems, his image will almost always be positive. A positive attitude by the chief is contagious and shows up in more courteous actions of company drivers and a smile on the face of the office trainee. If an army or a business enterprise really is to be seen as a team, each member must come to a sincere belief in the importance of his or her particular job. It has long been known in the military that the appearance of troops as they march by in a parade or the appearance of uniformed soldiers in town can reveal much about their attitude and the state of their weapons and training. In a business we recognize this immediately in the voice that answers the telephone or the service worker whose friendly behavior can bolster the efforts of the company salespeople by making sure that the goods get to the buyer on time and in good fashion.

Strength and the Decision Point

Some writers seem to believe that the execution of strategy (in contrast to its planning) is out of the hands of the strategist and is all in the hands of the troops. The objectives have been assigned, resources have been allocated to subordinate units, and the commanders then take charge of the action. Even Helmuth von Moltke, the great German strategist of the Franco-Prussian War, held the view that a strategist could plan the operation, but the execution must be left to the local commander. However, there is one final act that can only be taken by the person at the top. It is the decision to commit the resources held in reserve. This action directly reflects a studied perception of the decisive point in a campaign—the place where one must be strongest in order to win. In either business or the military, this decision requires a willingness to commit all the remaining resources if necessary, and with this there is then no turning back. This decision must always be reserved for the senior commander.

There are those who argue that certain situations require the use of all resources while others may not. Napoleon had very definite ideas on this subject. He felt strongly that the decision to commit the reserve was not a matter of *if*, but rather one of *when*. To him, holding back unused resources meant creating a weakness in some area of the contest when strength may be needed most. In this sense, holding out a reserve for future action was justified only to ensure the maximum strength at the decisive point. In a military situation, this added force is the final shock agent and should be of such overwhelming power that the morale of the opponent is broken and that the opponent's will to continue is gone. When this is correctly accomplished (and any further resistance is cut short), fewer losses for friends, and enemies alike, will result.

The act of committing reserves in the business world may be somewhat less obvious than such a commitment is under wartime conditions. In the case where one of two competitors is gaining in reputation as a leader in price or quality, the well-timed introduction of a new product, a greater improvement in quality, or a drastic reduction in cost may have much the same effect as the committing of an army reserve. The ability to commit extra money to ensure an advantageous acquisition or an extra show of expertise that gains a critical contract are also prime examples. It is worth noting here that the expertise and personality of the chief executive may count as the greatest reserve of all. In any case, the timely decision to add more money and talent might slow down a weaker competitor or even convince the competitor to leave the market.

Turenne was admired and loved by kings and soldiers alike. In modern times we seem to hear less of such giants in warfare or in commerce, but the legends are there nonetheless. A story is told that Andrew Carnegie, on his deathbed in August 1919, asked to be handed his favorite photograph of his old colleague and close friend, Charlie Schwab. He looked at it and smiled then closed his eyes for the last time. Schwab had served Carnegie for forty years, and during that time he had been the chief executive of two of the largest steel companies in the United States. He had been one of the founders and the first president of U.S. Steel, and known internationally in his field.

Schwab was also known for an unusual ability to lead workers no matter what the project. After having entered World War I in 1917, the United States' need for ships was so great by April 1918 that schedules were falling behind and complaints were increasing daily about shortages of materials, poor workmanship, and a lack of effort in support of the war. As the situation continued to grow worse, the shipping board decided to recruit one of the top business executives in the nation to head the Emergency Fleet Corporation. Their first choice was Henry Ford, but he chose not to accept the appointment. The next choice was Charles M. Schwab, then chairman of Bethlehem Steel. After a personal interview by President Woodrow Wilson, Schwab accepted the job at the pay of $1.00 per year. A press release later said that because of Schwab's great experience as a steelmaker and shipbuilder, he had been drafted. *The Literary Digest* commented that "Schwab knows steel, knows ships, knows how to handle labor, and has the prestige which carries the weight with every businessman in the country." It is interesting to note how easily that statement could have been translated to read that Schwab "knows the job (task), the workers (group), and himself (leader), and these very elements guarantee that the job will get done." Less than two months after Schwab took charge of the shipbuilding operation, there was an increase in the number of ships being delivered, and by the fall of 1918, production at most plants was on or ahead of schedule. In September he reported to his old friend Carnegie that during the previous month they had put as many ships into commission as the entire United States had produced in a year before the war. Later, someone remarked that if Charles Schwab had died in 1918, he would have been given a state funeral.

Charles Schwab was admired by the lowest ranks of workers and the highest level of managers. Like Turenne, a fellow executive who had lived hundreds of years before him, Schwab could quickly comprehend the situation, create a credible strategy, and guide workers to success.

— 8 —

Mark the Progress and the Problems

The Mongols had already occupied Russia. Now they were pre-pared to drive further west. Once they began to move, they never looked back. In fact, they traveled so fast that local observers could not believe that the same group was at two different places in such a short time. Reports on their number soon became exag-gerated; the word *horde* (a Mongol tribe or field army) came to mean "relentless mass of humanity, an overwhelming throng."

It did not seem to make any difference that the Mongol armies were not large and were often outnumbered by the Europeans. By A.D. 1241, the armies of the Khan had invaded both Poland and Hungary and had given cause for fear and trembling in the other countries nearby. No defender or obstacle ever seemed able to stop them. One probable cause was that their strategy and combat in-telligence were far ahead of their time; the attention they gave to detail was unusual and sometimes quite unsettling.

If you had been privileged to visit the Mongol army headquar-ters during that time, one of the staff officers present might have explained to you about the strange bags that the couriers were carrying into the compound. This was an old mongol tradition and part of a reporting system. The routine was simple. After a battle was over, men were assigned to survey the field of action and lo-cate the enemy dead. From each one of these, the right ear was cut off, placed in a bag, and carried back for counting and reporting later as a record of enemy slain.

Emphasis was placed on accuracy and also on speed in reporting. Each Mongol outpost and field army contained elements that were part of a system of "arrow" messengers who carried news back to the Khan. This group of messengers consisted of specially chosen riders who literally slept in the saddle and rode a horse to exhaustion, if need be, to speed the messages through. When the bell on the mount of one of these riders was heard approaching, any person in the vicinity, including a prince of the realm, was expected to get out of the messenger's way without hesitation. If a horse was lost or too weary to continue, the commander of the local area was required to furnish a replacement immediately from the best of his own horses. It is not surprising that these riders routinely covered in days the distances that ordinary travelers could not hope to navigate in weeks.

Numbers Are Faster Than Words

To judge the amount of progress or the effects of any action, we must first describe what happened and do so as clearly as possible. The Mongols may have been unique in bagging the ears of their competitors as a means of gathering intelligence, but other armies have also worked to improve the accuracy and the speed of reporting. Napoleon always looked for a count of the battalions engaged, especially the number of soldiers or artillery. Helmuth von Moltke, the great Prussian chief of staff, paid close attention to precision in timing and engaged in careful calculations when the movement of troops was involved. Partly as a result of this, he became famous for his "reckon, then risk" approach to the conduct of war. In his, and many other cases, we see the lesson repeated: accuracy is always important in strategic planning or in execution. Precision demands that, wherever possible, numbers should always come first. Words have given inspiration since before the days of the Greeks, but there are also times to disagree with the simplified world of such classical comments as, "The Spartans are not wont to ask how many, but where the enemy are." Most successful strategists would like to know both—where and how many troops they are likely to encounter.

Environmental, organizational, and strategic conditions often can be described with either words or numbers, but there is simply less confusion when meaningful numbers are used. A report that an infantry company is advancing toward an objective two miles to its front is worth considerably more than a message that there is "a little bit further to go." With numbers, the arguments are settled more quickly; the situation is easier to judge. As stated by one old soldier, "In fighting a war of words, a rifle is better than a shotgun."

While numbers do give a greater sense of exactness, they also give rise to other issues that need to be resolved. First, attention must be given to the types of numbers involved. Numbers refer to many different things, and some numbers are more useful than others. The question really boils down to what is being measured.

One definition of *measurement* is "the act of assigning numbers, guided by some stated rule." For example, a number may be used to substitute for a name or a part of a name. I can identify myself by a word (my name) or by my Social Security number. I can show the place where I live by giving the city and street names and adding the number of the house. We can each be viewed as a telephone number, a credit card number, or even a football jersey number. Numbers can also be used to describe different groups of objects or certain types of events. In a military unit, the soldiers checked off as "Present-Yes" may be indicated by a "1," while others checked as "Present-No" are simply listed as "0." In this system, the size of a unit can be given by stating the number of those "Present-Yes." We could also list their personal identity numbers with others that show their ranks (e.g., Airman First, Second, Third, etc.).

We are all familiar with descriptions where words are combined with numbers (e.g., 20 shares of stock $\times$ \$40 a share = \$800 stock value), but there are also cases where different types of numbering systems can make this practice misleading. One has to be careful to decide sometimes whether we are dealing with measurements that are actually quantifiable or whether they are merely ordered. For example, a person who scores 120 on a standard intelligence test cannot be said to be twice as smart as one who scores only 60. Human behavior is not quite so simple. All we can really say, in this case, is that one score (IQ 120) is higher than the other (IQ 60) on the scale that is being used. The description might actually be more clearly understood if it were only stated in words (i.e., first rank, second rank, third rank, etc.), since many of the numbers we can apply to human characteristics are no better than names or rankings (as in the grades A, B, C, or 1st, 2nd, 3rd, etc.). There are exceptions to this rule, such as weight, height, temperature, but certainly not very many. It is true that Person A can be described as weighing twice as much as Person B, or as being 1.5 times as tall, because weight and height or distance use a different (interval) numbering system. On the other hand, no one has yet found numbers to prove that A is twice as good-looking (or half as worthy of trust) as B. In most such cases of human description, we depend on a form of judgment that gives us only rankings or simply takes the opinion of an individual we choose to consider an expert. Often, the best description we can agree on is yes or no, given numbers 1 or 0 respectively. In many types of decision making, that measure can be determined by a single critical factor.

Spirits Both Strong and Subtle

With all the information at hand, clear methods need to be used when one is deciding on courses of action. One simple solution to this problem is for one to take a blank sheet of paper (or a computer screen) and draw a line down the middle. On the left side one could write *for,* and on the right *against.* A greater number of items ending up on one side helps to speed up the making of the choices. While this seems easy enough, it does not solve all the problems. In the early stages of the United States' involvement in South Vietnam, the South Vietnamese Army was trying to help isolated mountaineer tribes defend themselves against Viet Cong guerrillas by offering weapons and training to people in secluded villages. In one case, the soldiers had hiked to a settlement in the jungle and a discussion was in progress. On the *for* side of the mental checklist about whether to set up a defensive project in the village were the following: 1) the village elders were interested in the project, 2) the weapons, training personnel, and air transport were available, 3) light aircraft could bring in the necessary items to an unimproved airstrip, and 4) a likely landing field was near the village, a flat section of ground that needed only the clearing of scattered vegetation. There appeared to be nothing on the *against* side of the ledger until the discussion turned to how to clear trees and shrubs. Even then no major difficulties arose except about one old tree in the middle of the open area. The soldiers thought it might take some extra effort—certainly not very much, but at this point the villagers balked. Why? The tree could not be disturbed. Why not? The village spirit lived in the tree. *Stop.* Whatever your views on village spirits may be, one item outweighed all the other factors, and the entire project was scratched.

Vietnamese soldiers and mountain tribemembers are not the only decision-makers who must look for critical factors. Some years ago, when *computers* meant big machines that took up an air-conditioned room, one of the large technology companies in the United States decided to go head-to-head with IBM, which then held about 70 percent of the market. The logic of the high-tech firm was that it had outstanding scientists, engineers, and technicians who were nearly the best in the industry; they estimated that they could build computers as good as or perhaps even better than those built by any existing competitor. The general consensus at the time was that they were probably right. So, start the list on the *for* side. The chief executive announced that his company would enter the market with the intention, in a very few years, of becoming second only to IBM (there were several other companies that sought to compete in the market). Unfortunately, not too many years had passed before the company had changed its mind and had decided to quit the computer business with a loss of nearly $500 million. What had happened? They seemed with all their science and engineering expertise to be as good as they claimed to be on the *for* side, but they failed to list some critical items on the other side, such as whether IBM's customers would want to make the switch. Actually, Big Blue's reputation was such ("After the sale, we hold their hand") that most customers were already satisfied. The talent that the new contender had was on the side of operations; that talent was not matched by power in the market. The "village spirit" factor had made its point again, outweighing a more impressive kind of easy-to-see advantage. The case is only one more reminder that decisions in complex situations depend not only on the kind of information available but also on the context in which the problem occurs. Techniques for screening and transmitting information can generate volumes of data, but the first and most basic questions are how such data are related to the other items and where the data rank on the scale of values. Even though the very best of computers might be available, that judgment is best made by a human being.

How Do You Measure Success?

Everyone starts early in life with such questions as "What do they think of me?" and "Where do I stand in my group?" Each person wants to know if she can really run faster than someone else or whether his team will be first in the race. One thing most of us can agree on—we don't like being uncertain. A military organization looks for ways to judge its own potential and how it would fare in a war. A business is much the same: it makes a reasonable profit or hazards the prospect of failure. In real life, the standard by which we are all measured is that of the clan-village hunter: it is either a win or a loss. The question has always been: How do we measure success?

The military has speculated for a long time about how the effectiveness of a combat unit can be measured (e.g., by the number of square miles of enemy territory captured). Would a good standard be enemy casualties? Is a business enterprise best described by the value of its sales or by its assets? How about profit or loss? With measures in use today, we show only a few of the characteristics of any individual or group; many of those we commonly use are not as good as they seem to be. While the dollar value of an increase in sales would seem to be reasonable enough in estimating business improvement, the truth may partly escape us. The change could be due to inflation; the numbers increased from the years before, but the value continues unchanged.

Despite our pessimism about the problem of accuracy, and however we choose to describe our strengths or weaknesses, more numbers can help in the process. If the customers, workers, investors, and the public are all convinced that the published data show our corporation to be near the best, the chances are greatly increased that it will be given high standing.

Actually, we know the first requisite for strategic success; it is capability, the total of various means or resources that set the upper limits on what we can hope to achieve. When an army commander comes to the realization that he lacks enough combat strength to win, the contest is over at that moment—though there still may be thousands of soldiers ready with loaded rifles in hand. In much of modern warfare, the first decline in combat ability comes with a loss of fire superiority (in business, read "product" or "market share") and worsens with limits on movement. Reserve units are not shifted as quickly, and supplies do not arrive as they should at the proper place or on time. In a day of relentless air strikes, the major resource installations (factories, communications centers, supply points, etc.) cannot be repaired soon enough, and, as the flow of information is interrupted, coordination is increasingly difficult. When new ground is not being taken, priorities begin to change, first to holding the present position, then to reducing the loss. Increasing numbers of individuals give up, followed later by entire units, surrendering intact. As the sequence to failure runs its course, it is easy to guess what went wrong, but now it is poor consolation. The real problem is much further back: a question of whether the potential for failure could have been recognized sooner, before the downturn began. We often find out too late: soothsaying is a difficult business.

In attempting to solve this problem of foresight, it is natural that many practitioners will try to work mostly with numbers. This is understandable; humans are measuring animals. Not only are we always curious; we are constantly asking to know how much or how many of this or that, which one is the better of two, and what was it that came before now. The evaluation of factors in strategy is so complex that one is tempted to say it probably cannot be done. But that is not really an option; we have no choice but to try.

Whatever approach is taken to strategy, the questions are still much the same: what are the best signs of opportunity or threat in the environment, the strengths and weaknesses of the organization, and the positive or negative results of actions. In any military or business situation, we need a list of factors that seem to promise success.

If we follow the logic of the battlefield, we quickly guess that a combat unit with artillery and other types of fire support will have the best chance to move forward. But, when trying to test this hypothesis, we find ourselves searching again for reliable measures of firepower. In judging ability to move large numbers of troops or volumes of arms and supplies, we face more measurement problems. We would like to have more details, for instance, on the status of motor, rail, water, or air transportation that is available. But even more important is the number of combat-ready vehicles and the number of troops they can move. The Franco-Prussian War of 1870 gives a classic example. In just fifteen days, with a detailed knowledge of troop strengths and rail nets, Moltke moved three Prussian field armies into position to overrun the French defenses before they could muster their forces.

The critical factors in a situation must be clearly identified and always considered together. These factors are, in many respects, like the various elements that make up a human being; we cannot expect to describe an individual in terms of only one feature. It is equally unrealistic to think of an organization in terms of a single dimension. Just as the human personality is a complex of many actions and attributes, the organization is a group of various individuals that perform various functions and yet are part of a whole.

The complex of different factors may be seen as separate items but must be studied in interaction.

Thinking the Pieces Together

The knowledge problem for the chief executive is one of how to keep track of the whole operation while not forgetting its elements. To some dirty-nail practitioners, it may come as a bit of a shock when we say that one of the best ways to do this is to theorize. There are still too many managers today who see theory as something you tolerate in college and promptly forget at graduation. This is a big mistake. Probably the worst thing about theory is its name. It is only a collection of ideas that someone puts together so they make better sense. Theory is simply a way to help us organize thinking. If we know the key elements of a business (or an army), and we see how they fit together, we are already using a theory, regardless of how we describe it.

Information processing is an area that none of us can ignore, and the habit of good theorizing may be our most valuable helpmate. The best way to proceed in theorizing is probably to make it all up as you go—here is one way we can start.

$$PAST \rightarrow PRESENT \rightarrow FUTURE$$

We already know the elements; we also know their relationships. Not so complex, is it? Better not be so sure. Anyone can guess from the diagram above that knowledge of the past will help us to understand the present and maybe give us clues to the future. But now, shift things around a little and try to add just a few elements.

$$FUTURE\ (NORTH)$$
$$\uparrow$$
$$INFORMATION\ (WEST) \rightarrow PRESENT \leftarrow INFORMATION\ (EAST)$$
$$\uparrow$$
$$PAST\ (SOUTH)$$

Here, we have an outline (or map-read theory) that we might call the compass model. It now indicates that we need information from the past and also from other areas to make the most sense of the present. All of these elements then help us in making more sense of the future. If we adopt some business terminology, the diagram may become very useful.

OUR COMPANY—
FUTURE
(TEN YEARS ON)
↑

COMPETITOR W → OUR COMPANY ← COMPETITOR E
PRESENT   PRESENT   PRESENT
↑

OUR COMPANY—
PAST
(FIVE YEARS AGO)

The compass model gives us a simple framework from which to develop our checklists to make comparisons with conditions as they were in the past, what they are in the present, and what may be in the future. It is only a short step from here to designing a "War Room" or other type of operations center that can be used with situation maps and background information for more detailed evaluations or for anticipating new problems. We might rather name this a Competitor System Center (CSC), instead of a battlefield War Room, to better describe its activity. In any case, the walls of the center could be used for charts (or computer-displayed spreadsheets) describing the current situation, estimates, and likely projections.

A Strategic Management Matrix (SMM)

A military or business organization is driven by so many different forces that it is easy to become discouraged from attempting a careful analysis. The best thing to do, as one old saying goes, is to start at the beginning.

In judging aspects of a major enterprise, we can start by trying to see 1) the scope of its present environment, 2) the resources available to it, 3) the enterprise's past actions and its range of experience, 4) the objectives it has pursued in the past, and 5) the results obtained by its efforts. When these elements are studied in comparable groups, they emphasize the functions of general management, the major resources assembled, and the operations that match the resources. They will also be found to be in constant interaction and to be increasing the range of their contacts.

One way to visualize the parts of this puzzle is to build up a matrix of impacts. For a business, items from the areas of information-collecting, operations, administration or command, personnel, and logistics are placed in a single diagram to highlight their interactions. The matrix can serve as a visual checklist that can be of help to us in considering the range of capabilities or possible courses of action. See Table 8.1.

After checking the General Environment (or theater of operations), the chief executive should narrow the focus more to the industry area (or battlefield) and the important competitors. Then, in the central part of the matrix, he or she should move to a complex of elements concerning the organization and strategy. In the first column (Resource) are notations on the means available. In the second column (Action) are items related to change. In the third column (Objectives) we see factors that indicate purpose.

From a somewhat different perspective (by rows), the cells can emphasize tactics. In the top row, we focus on information, its collection and use. The second row points us to operations. The third row orients us toward matters of general management and integrative activities (e.g., plans or control). The fourth row draws attention to personnel actions and problems. The fifth row concerns finance.

The section called Results can be subdivided into two basic formats: the short-term effects and the long-term effects. For successful short-term outcomes, a general must win the battles; for successful long-term results, he must end the war with a victory.

The Strategic Management Matrix can easily become a checklist. The first cell (row one and column one—Market Data), reflects

Strategic Management Matrix
(Critical Business Factors)

	Environment		Organization/Strategy			Results	
	(General)	(Special)	(Resource)	(Action)	(Objective)	(Short-Term)	(Long-Term)
Marketing			Information availability	Sales gains	Maximum sales		
Operations			Know-how availability	Quality improvement	Minimum costs		
CEO	General economic condition	Industry condition	Management availability	Administrative improvement	Integrative effort	Return on total assets	Market value
Personnel			Worker availability	Method improvement	Employee morale		
Finance			Financial availability	Asset gains	Investor income		

an information resource—in a military situation, combat intelligence. The next cell in the same row describes an activity (e.g., forward observation), and the rightmost cell shows a particular objective (e.g., information on enemy dispositions).

In the second row, we look at the elements of operations. A basic resource is the fighting unit, the action is training and combat, and the objective is to seize and control terrain.

The third row would be of direct concern to the commander or chief executive. Here there might be items on the availability of good leaders (always a critical resource), general methods and policy, and overall direction of effort.

In the fourth row, the resource is always manpower, the actions could be better training, and an objective could be to maximize strength. In the fifth row, the key resource is money or material, actions are designed to improve the organization's status, and an objective might be to improve overall readiness.

One concern in using the matrix is in keeping the display understandable. Words seem to be the best way to do this initially, but we also have a need for numbers. To describe the overall business environment, economic researchers often try to use some form of "leading" indicator, a composite number or index used to highlight present conditions or conditions that could come up in the future.

For special sections of the environment (e.g., an industry or market sector), one might use numbers that show the weekly rankings of various industry activities. A high rating (an industry expected to be more active in coming months) could suggest an improving economy.

Ratios are frequently used to show competitor characteristics or give other clues about that competitor's strategy. In the section on marketing information, an estimate of resources might be obtained from public data on research or advertising. In operations, the levels of cash and inventories are examples of useful data. In the cells describing finance, the use of numbers is almost habitual. Resource capability is shown in different asset values and in various descriptions of debt. Typical actions or allocations can be estimated by items and their interactions (e.g., inventory vs. total sales), and suggestions about whether the objectives (e.g., strength in financial position) are being reached can also show up in ratios (e.g., debt vs. equity, etc.).

In the results section of the matrix, ratios are in common use. One is the relationship of income to total assets, or return on assets, a measure of short-term performance. For the longer term, a case is sometimes made taking a look at the market value of the company stock (the stock price multiplied by the number of common shares outstanding) compared to its total assets. This ratio shows how much investors are willing to pay for shares in the firm, compared to the value of its assets. Stated another way, it is an indication of how much the stock market is willing to pay for the efforts of company management.

By preparing a matrix reflecting each competitor as well as a matrix reflecting the subject company, executives can make industry comparisons on an ongoing basis. These comparisons, combined with reports on the company's past and its future, can give a more integrated picture of the company's mission and where it is projected to be going. If the picture is carefully painted, it helps much with the strategy puzzle.

Still More Rivers to Cross

The chief executive of a business organization is commonly cast in either one of two roles. Sometimes, a person is the captain of a sinking merchant ship; more often, he or she is the principal dancer or lead in a classical ballet. As the ship's unfortunate captain, they must keep the bilge pumps running at full speed while trying to decide what must be jettisoned in order to increase the chance of survival. All the while, the captain is trying to salvage any cargo that can be sold whenever the boat reaches the harbor. In business terms, the captain must first cut costs until they match income, then work at increasing sales. One of the many problems is that the workers may be let go, and the captain is many times uncertain whether he or she is losing the best or the worst. The same can often be said about the products that are selected. Both sides of this dilemma are basically problems in value.

As the principal ballet dancer, the chief must not only match efforts to those of the other performers, but also has the daunting task of establishing rapport with audience members who come from various backgrounds. In a business environment, he or she must bear with fellow competitors while the major thrust of their effort is to understand customers, workers, investors, and others in the community. To discover just what these many interests might be is another problem in measurement where answers are hard to obtain. Whatever the role he or she is cast in, there always seem a thousand questions with educated guesses for answers.

The Mongols' obsession with careful staff work and accurate, prompt reporting paid off most handsomely for them on many important occasions. No European army was ever able to match the violent horsemen throughout their drive to the west. By the end of A.D. 1241, they had defeated the armed forces of Poland and Hungary and had started to move further west. Fate would cause this to change. As they drove toward Italy and southern Europe, the invaders were suddenly halted—they had received a critical message.

The laws laid down by Genghis Khan were very strict. One of these required all of the senior commanders, upon receiving notice of the Khan's death, to return to the capital at Karakorum to elect a new Khan. In A.D. 1242, the generals of the hordes from the Gobi, who were at the outskirts of Vienna and on the borders of northern Italy, got word that the reigning Khan, Ogatai, was dead. Their action was very simple; they turned armies around and rode back to the land they had come from, 6,000 miles to the east. They never returned to the west. The Mongols' mission had changed.

The modern-day executive—and the ancient Samurai swordsman—would understand the situation.

Some Military-Business Maxims

General

Look at the big picture first.

Hannibal, before the battle of Cannae, told his troops to expect that in the early stages of the battle the center would be driven back by the Romans. But in doing this, the Romans would crowd themselves together and become vulnerable to a counterattack. According to Hannibal's plan, the Carthaginian center would give way in an orderly fashion while the troops on the flanks held in place. When the Romans were fully committed, the Carthaginian troops in the center slowed their retreat, then held firm while the others attacked from both sides. The Romans were completely and hopelessly surrounded. Hannibal thus destroyed an army that was twice the size of his own.

According to Thomas J. Watson, Jr., much of the early success of IBM was due to what was called "systems" thinking. Competitors did not seem to understand that IBM offered more than just machinery. Many companies entered the field with better hardware and then failed to properly install and service it. They then often lost customers to IBM. The IBM approach was a conscious integration of products and service combined with a belief that the customer is key to success.

Environment

Don't leave anything out.

The first item on the list of instructions from Robert Rogers to his Rangers during the French and Indian War was, "Don't forget nothing." The instructions are still a part of the training of U.S. Army Rangers today.

An important meeting at General Motors is said to have been adjourned by Alfred Sloan because no one could think of an objection to a proposal that had been presented. Sloan then announced that the committee would meet again after they had had time to consider what might have been overlooked. At the second meeting, a number of questions were asked and the proposal was disapproved. Sloan apparently did not feel obliged to remind the committee members that sometimes things that are left out can be more important than those that are included.

Look for what causes change.

Change can present us with more opportunities and with even greater risks. Past history is one pattern of good clues to what may happen tomorrow. The past can foretell the present, and the present can foretell the future. The mission determines key objectives, and these guide resources and actions. We must try to anticipate what could possibly happen and then guess how it would affect strategy.

Robert Woods of Sears, Roebuck and Co. spent considerable time studying population patterns in the United States. He saw a shift from the farm to the town, a new and different market for his company. There is always a need to find out what new inventions or products can make existing ones obsolete. Trends in the mix of the data and cultural changes can alter the threats and opportunities.

Organization

Be ready to deal with the worst.

This is a crude paraphrase of Sun Tzu's observation that the good fighters of old first put themselves beyond the possibility of defeat. Only when they were satisfied with these preparations did they begin to make other plans for battle.

Some companies try to start a project without first making certain that it will last out the first critical months (or years). The managers of any firm who enter a new market unprepared to cope with minimum sales are obviously courting disaster. When adverse conditions occur, the odds increase that the venture will fail.

Make sure that the mission is clear.

The mission, or general purpose, of an organization has both 1) tangible aspects and 2) intangible aspects. In a military situation, the artillery's mission is to provide 1) firepower (quite tangible) and 2) flexibility (intangible) on the battlefield. The infantry offers 1) close combat capability (tangible) and 2) decisiveness (intangible). The intangible elements, especially, must be as clear as possible.

The mission of a business organization includes 1) the provision of a tangible product or service to a customer and 2) the creation of an intangible image in the minds of contributors. A computer company might provide 1) computers at low cost that 2) are of good quality; while another firm might 1) offer very low-priced watches that 2) may be thrown away after use. It is essential that both aspects of the mission be clearly understood by the customer, the worker, the investor, and others involved with the firm.

Publish a list of priorities.

Priorities are a help in emphasizing the key areas assigned for operations and its resources that can be expected to be available.

The objectives provide guides for action, but resources provide the means. Attack orders for combat specify which units will have additional supporting units attached to them for the operation, and which units will receive priority for artillery and mortar fire support.

In a business, when no priorities are stated, the presumption must be that any one project is as important as any other and that the most persuasive argument (or presentation) for more money or increased operations will prevail. Depending on the motivation of subordinate managers, the emphasis can soon become one of "empire building," and greater consumption of scarce resources instead of the employment of greater efficiency.

Strategy

Assign objectives, not actions.

Strategy is the method by which the mission is accomplished. Accomplishing the mission is its only purpose. From an overall viewpoint, the strategy becomes a pattern of actions that describe the dynamic aspects of the whole organization when that organization is directed toward key objectives and is supported by available resources. Coordination is an essential part of this effort and is in the interest of every participant. Ideally, opinions about the mission have been sought from every level, every aspect of the mission has been considered, and the parts of the enterprise coincide with the whole. There are, of course, hazards in trying to keep minds open. Frederick the Great made it a special point to note that it is difficult to obtain unbiased comments if subordinates think the commander has already made up his mind.

A movie version of the executive seems to stress the need to get "facts," but Peter Drucker and others have noted the important role of opinions. In one sense, they are a measure of creative thinking; each person takes the same set of facts into his own mental framework and builds up his personal viewpoint—often a new arrangement of the separate pieces of data.

Focus on the critical few.

The term *essential elements of information* is used to describe items that are important to decision making in a military operation. Not only are there certain analytical factors that are important in making a decision, there are always some critical junctures in space and time that determine success or failure. One hill or a single outpost can hold up an advance; one bridge can cost or save many lives.

C. I. Barnard referred to the "limiting factors" in a given situation. He cited the example of one missing screw that could disable a piece of machinery. In business, there may be a gap in technology that cannot be breached or a single item of information that could cost a company a sale.

Communication

Be certain they all get the word.

If those at the end of the communication chain have a clear understanding of what is to be done, and why, it is much more likely that those in between have also received the message. Time must be allocated for orientation sessions and many questions. If there is too little time, it may mean that there is little deliberation and probably a lack of effective feedback. Good commanders spend much time in the field, and they spend less time at the headquarters or at the rear.

Hewlett-Packard's "management by walking around" is a business equivalent of this practice.

Actions (of the Chief)

Go to the sound of the guns.

The best commander goes to where the decisive action will take place. This is one more application of the fundamental law of strategy: Be stronger at the decisive point. The senior commander personalizes the support capability and decision making on all of the available resources that can be focused on a particular place and time. He is at the key point in the operation where the major action is expected and the reserves will be committed.

This could be the point in a business operation where one firm has an opportunity to jump ahead of competitors. Timex could have grabbed the digital watch market but did not; Motorola decided against transistors and lost ground. On the other hand, Johnson & Johnson promptly recalled Tylenol when the company's reputation was threatened and quickly recovered its place in the market. Both the talent of the chief executive and the analysis of business conditions must be good enough that the critical point in the situation is recognized. The chairman of Exxon came to regret that he did not go to the scene of the action when a major oil spill *(Valdez)* occurred. He had been persuaded by his staff that he had better communication at his headquarters, but that decision turned out to be wrong. When the news reporters got to the scene, there was no senior company management personnel present to clarify guesses and rumors.

Results

Mark the progress and the problems.

Military intelligence officers insist that information be verified by at least two different sources. Any commander should do at least as much in evaluating the performance of one of his units. But first the difference between good or bad performance must be established. Given that, he should then look for multiple descriptors in order to obtain the clearest possible picture of the situation so that better judgments can be made. We do well to remember Sun Tzu's advice to do "many calculations" before we come to decide.

Good accountants double check the calculations they make. Chief executives should do no less. A business corporation must always be evaluated from many different angles. Customers and their interests can be judged by sales, investors by return, workers by the amount of pay and benefits, and so on. When all the many aspects have been accounted for, the organization as a whole can be considered.

Learn from everyone else.

Napoleon once said, "Read over and over the campaigns of Alexander, Hannibal, Caesar, Gustavus, Turenne, Eugene, and Frederick. Make them your models. This is the only way to become a great general and to master the secrets of the art of war."

There have also been many talented businesspeople with important lessons for us all. A short list of old timers could include T. M. Vail, Charles M. Schwab, Henry Ford, Alfred Sloan, Robert E. Wood, Thomas Watson, and many others.

Finally, it is worth remembering that we can often learn much more from a few things we do wrong than we can from many things we do right. What we really learn from such experience is 1) why we made the mistake, and 2) how to avoid it next time. Someone long ago once said, "It doesn't matter so much how many times we fall down. The question is whether we get up to try it over again."

Bibliography

Andrews, K. R. *The Concept of Corporate Strategy.* Homewood, IL: Dow Jones-Irwin, 1971.

Anthony, R. N. *Planning and Control Systems: A Framework for Analysis.* Boston, MA: Graduate School of Business Administration, Harvard University, 1965.

Ardant du Picq, Charles. *Battle Studies: Ancient and Modern Battle.* Harrisburgh, PA: Military Service Publishing, 1946.

Barnard, C. I. *The Functions of the Executive.* Cambridge, MA: Harvard University Press, 1968.

Burne, A. H. *The Art of War on Land.* Harrisburgh, PA: Military Service Publishing, 1947.

Chambers, J. *The Devil's Horsemen.* London: Cassell Publishers, Ltd., 1988.

Chandler, A. D., Jr. *Strategy and Structure.* Cambridge, MA: MIT Press, 1962.

Drucker, P. *The Practice of Management.* New York: Harper & Row, 1954.

Fox, E. M., & L. Urwick. *Dynamic Administration: The Collected Works of Mary Parker Follett.* New York: Hippocrene Books, Inc., 1973.

Glueck, W. F., & L. R. Jauch. *Business Policy and Strategic Management.* New York: McGraw-Hill, 1984.

Hart, B. H. L. *Strategy.* 2d ed. New York: NAL Penguin, 1967.

Hessen, R. *Steel Titan.* Pittsburgh, PA: University of Pittsburgh Press, 1975.

Hofer, C. W., & D. Schendel. *Strategy Formulation.* St. Paul, MN: West Publishing, 1978.

Jomini, H. *The Art of War.* Westport, CT: Greenwood Press, 1971.

Musashi, M. *A Book of Five Rings.* Woodstock, NY: The Overlook Press, 1974.

Phillips, T. R., ed. *Roots of Strategy.* Harrisburgh, PA: Military Service Publishing, 1940.

Swinton, E. D. *The Defense of Duffer's Drift.* Wayne, NY: Avery Publishing Group, 1986.

Turnbull, R. *Battles of the Samurai.* London: Arms and Armour Press, 1987.

Wartenburg, C. Y. von. *Napoleon as a General.* Vol. 1. The Wolseley Series. London: Gilbert and Rivington, 1897.

Weygand, M. *Turenne, Marshal of France.* Boston, MA: Houghton Mifflin, 1930.

————. *Department of the Army Field Manual FM 101–5, Staff Organization & Procedure.* Washington, D.C.: U.S. Government Printing Office, 1954.

————. *Department of the Army Field Manual FM 100–5, Operations.* Washington, D.C.: U.S. Government Printing Office, 1944.

————. *Jomini, Clausewitz and Schlieffen.* West Point, NY: U.S. Military Academy, 1943.

————. *Summaries of Selected Military Compaigns.* West Point, NY: U.S. Military Academy, 1953.